METS STORIES I ONLY TELL MY FRIENDS

Art Shamsky
and
Matthew Silverman

TRIUMPH
BOOKS

Copyright © 2025 by Art Shamsky and Matthew Silverman

No part of this publication may be reproduced, stored in a retrieval system, or transmitted in any form by any means, electronic, mechanical, photocopying, or otherwise, without the prior written permission of the publisher, Triumph Books LLC, 814 North Franklin Street, Chicago, Illinois 60610.

Library of Congress Cataloging-in-Publication Data available upon request.

This book is available in quantity at special discounts for your group or organization. For further information, contact:

Triumph Books LLC
814 North Franklin Street
Chicago, Illinois 60610
(312) 337–0747
www.triumphbooks.com

Printed in U.S.A.
ISBN: 978–1–63727–709–6
Design by Nord Compo

All photographs courtesy of the authors unless otherwise noted.

This book is dedicated to my dad, Bill,
who started playing catch with me as soon as I could walk.
He introduced me to the wonderful game of baseball.
In some small way I hope I made him proud.
—A.S.

CONTENTS

FOREWORD

I know what you're thinking: *What can possibly be said or written about the 1969 world champion New York Mets that hasn't been already?* This book is the answer to that question, and in an odd twist, its genesis owes to none other than former World War II general and, later, United States president Dwight D. Eisenhower, known to the world as Ike.

Ike actually passed away in March 1969, before the historic Mets season, but earlier in that decade, in 1967, he published a book titled *At Ease: Stories I Tell to Friends*. When Art Shamsky—a key member of the 1969 championship Mets team and the author of this book—learned of Eisenhower's tome decades later, he had an epiphany: he would do something similar and reveal a cache of previously untold Mets stories. Everyone has heard about Tom Seaver's near-perfect game, manager Gil Hodges's impact on the team, the black cat that visited the Chicago Cubs during a key September game at Shea Stadium, and several other "standards," but Art had so many more fun, intimate stories stored away in his mind's vault that he was inspired to put many of them on the record to share with us for the first time.

I've known Art for a long time, and I'm proud and honored to call him a friend. He might have told one or two of these stories to me over the years, but all they did was whet my appetite for more. In fact, think of this book as one long, delicious dinner during which you will read about: how much Art and Gil actually spoke during their time together, how Art wound up on the cover of a famous national magazine with a well-known supermodel, tales of various nights on the town with good pal and teammate Ken Boswell, fun and games with Tug McGraw, the aftermath of the 1969 Mets' epochal World Series win, and so much more. A better dinner companion you will not find.

This book is not exclusively based on the 1969 world championship. It delves into Art's career before and after becoming a Met; his days as a sportscaster in the late 1980s, during which we worked together at the fledgling all-sports radio station WFAN in New York; his experience with helping develop baseball in Israel; and so much more.

I've always thought of Art as something of a renaissance man. He has worked tirelessly under often-difficult business circumstances to galvanize his former teammates, creating many opportunities to stay in the public eye and perpetuate the legacy of one of the most beloved teams in sports history. He has written other books, and he enjoyed a long broadcasting career on television and radio in New York; he continues to make appearances designed to educate younger fans about what made the 1969 Mets in particular, and that time in New York (and the entire country), worthy of continued reflection and appreciation.

I have stated unabashedly over the years that the 1969 New York Mets provided me with the happiest memory of my youth; I was 15 years old that year. But as is always the case, the ensuing five and a half decades have taken from us not only a number of players and staff from that team but many of those fans who were similarly in love with and impacted by the team. I recognize now that there are a couple generations of fans who "weren't there" and who need to hear the stories about who those Mets were, what they represented, and why they remain beloved today and will for eternity.

There is no better person to keep that flame burning than my friend Art Shamsky. I trust you will enjoy every story in this book. I know I will.

—Howie Rose
Broadcaster, New York Mets

INTRODUCTION

My life can be divided into two distinct parts: before 1969 and after 1969. And many things that have happened to me since then continue to tie in to that landmark year.

When Matt Silverman and I first talked about working together on a new project revolving around my time with the 1969 New York Mets, we both knew that we were not the first to tackle the subject. By our count, more books have been written about the world champion Mets of 1969 than any other team and year in sports history. That club is the ultimate underdog story. Given the deep roster of books dealing with that '69 season, we understood from the start that coming up with something different was definitely going to be a challenge.

Needless to say, New York Mets history itself is always interesting and sometimes laughable. And 1969 in particular has been dissected and explained in many books, including those written by both Matt and me. I have written two books that hinge on that year: *The Magnificent Seasons* (with Barry Zeman) and *After the Miracle* (coauthored by Erik Sherman).

Matt cowrote *The Miracle Has Landed* (with Ken Samelson and others) and authored several other books on the Mets, including *Shea Good-Bye* (with Keith Hernandez), *100 Things Mets Fans Should Know & Do Before They Die*, and *Mets Essential*, all from Triumph Books. One of the reasons there are so many books on the 1969 Mets is because fan interest on the subject has never waned. The early Mets teams and the 1969 season have a legacy that will live forever.

The success in 1969 increases the belly laughs when discussing the early inept years of the franchise that started in 1962. The Mets' unfathomable achievement in the fall of '69 justifies the previous missteps and false starts and provides insight into the turnaround that actually began in '68, Gil Hodges's first year as manager in New York—and my first year at Shea Stadium. We may have taken the world by surprise in '69, but that doesn't mean we hadn't been working hard behind a great manager and handler of men in Gil. We had a tremendous pitching staff grown through a solid farm system, and Gil and his dedicated coaches helped mold us into a cohesive unit. The '69 Mets utilized every player on the roster, improving as a team in increments and then by leaps and bounds starting in the latter part of August. In September and October 1969 we could not be stopped. The fans couldn't believe the change in fortune of a franchise that just a handful of years earlier had made Casey Stengel famously lament, "Can't anybody here play this game?"

So Matt and I wondered how we could pique readers' interest in yet another book about the 1969 Mets. We tossed around different ideas and spent a lot of time seeking answers. It always came back to, "It was already written about by someone before," or, "How many times can we write about the black cat, Ron

Swoboda's catch, and Tom Seaver's almost perfect game?" We were locked into trying to find an answer. While some ideas seemed to be worth pursuing, our overriding goal was to tell stories from a different angle or skip over the well-known in favor of something that was underappreciated or lost in the corners of history. It required a lot of digging, reworking, and rethinking. Maybe that's the price of being part of a team and a year that live on forever!

The beginning of the idea for this book started, however, when I read good friend and former public relations director for the New York Yankees Marty Appel's book titled *Pinstripes by the Tale: Half a Century in and Around Yankees Baseball.* Marty has written 26 books and has mastered the art of writing sports books. *Pinstripes by the Tale* is a book about Marty's years before, during, and after his time with the Yankees. He writes about people he met along the way and things that happened behind the scenes that most people have never heard about. After reading Marty's book, I realized there were things that happened to me that I was involved in that hadn't been written about—at least not in firsthand detail from me—that readers might enjoy.

Matt and I discussed the idea with our literary agent, Rob Wilson, who thought publishers might like the idea. A few days later Rob called me and mentioned a book by former US president Dwight D. Eisenhower that was published in 1967 titled *At Ease: Stories I Tell to Friends.* That phone call with Rob hit the right buttons and planted the seeds for this book. I started thinking about the books I have written and all the interviews I have conducted for other people's books, plus all the radio, television, magazine, and newspaper pieces I've done, and I realized there were many stories I hadn't detailed in any way. There were a lot of stories I hadn't thought about in years but that I felt were worth sharing.

Yes, the seeds were planted; now Matt and I had to figure out how to make them grow. We were both excited about the prospect, but being excited was the easy part; the follow-through would be a different story. But at least we had an idea!

That is how this book evolved. Matt and I tried not to be redundant with certain stories and events, but if there is something in here that you have heard or read about before, I hope what we have written adds a new twist or a more personal side to your understanding of the story. Anything mentioned more than once in the book is generally used as a reminder or—such as an abridged version of my sitting out the doubleheader on Rosh Hashanah in September 1969, for example—to give a different perspective on my professional relationship with Gil Hodges.

A few stories go back to my early years and my seasons before I was traded to the Mets from the Cincinnati Reds in the winter of 1967. That trade was shocking at first, but it forever changed my life. Looking back, I am so grateful for all the experiences I've had and people I have met. I am also thankful my memory proved strong and I was able to recall as much as I have. Do I have regrets? Of course! What is life without regrets? But mostly my life on and off the field with the Mets, and the subsequent years out of baseball, has been wonderful. But we have written about some regrets here. Teams decide to send you elsewhere, businesses slow down, and the world hands you your unconditional release now and again. New opportunities are often born of what once felt like despair.

I am truly thankful to be able to share the stories in this book with you, the reader. Our intention was simply to write about events and other things that are new to you or to which we have added a different twist. We hope you enjoy. Because truthfully, these are stories I would only tell to friends!

Chapter 1

LANDING IN NEW YORK

A National League City

I always heard that New York was a National League city. You had two teams—the Giants and the Dodgers—and they collectively had more fans than the Yankees, even though the Yankees had all those great seasons. After the Giants and Dodgers left for California in 1958, I think that their fans' allegiance carried over to the new National League club, the Mets. I saw this as a visiting player when I came to the major leagues with the Reds. Yes, I signed some autographs in Cincinnati as I left the park, but my first experience of seeing lines of autograph seekers camped out at our hotel was in New York when we came to play the Mets.

At the Roosevelt Hotel, where the Reds stayed in Manhattan, there were always 15 to 20 kids and others lined up to have us sign something. This was the mid-1960s, before anybody thought signatures on cards or memorabilia would ever be valuable. But it was New York. Before I knew it, I was seeing these fans every day on the streets of the city.

It's Not the Yankees . . . It's the Mets

How I wound up with the New York Mets in 1968 has its origins in the previous year, just before spring training. This story also illustrates how ballplayers were on their own before the advent of agents. It was like a one-way street, with the player waiting at the light, hoping to cross, and having only a few seconds to get across alive.

I had been with the Cincinnati Reds organization since they signed me in 1959, when I was just 17 years old (I didn't get called up to the majors until 1965). I spent the off-season in St. Louis, my hometown, and a week before spring training in 1967, I flew to Cincinnati to try to negotiate my contract after what I felt had been a successful second season in the majors. Of course, I had to pay for my flight.

We'd been going back and forth mailing letters to negotiate a contract. I was making $8,500, which was $1,500 more than the minimum salary. I'd just hit 21 home runs in around 230 at-bats. Only one other Red had more homers than me in 1966: Deron Johnson, who hit 24 in 500-plus at-bats. I made my case about hitting all those home runs despite so few at-bats, and the front office came right back with all these things to use against me. Reds general manager Bob Howsam wouldn't budge on $8,500 per year. I figured there was not much else I could do, and I decided to leave.

Howsam said, "Before you go, I see that your second daughter was born in January." Our meeting was sometime around the end of February. And he said, "We have a gift for you and your family." He gave me an envelope, which I put in my pocket. On the airplane home, I opened the envelope, and there was a note. It read, "In honor of your child being born, here is a gift from the Cincinnati Reds." It was a US savings bond for $18.75, which matured to $25 in however many years it took to mature.

Back in those days, you had to be careful. If you became a problem, or were perceived by ownership as a "loose cannon," you might find yourself somewhere else. That wasn't the case with me: I got hurt in 1967 and went from 21 home runs to 3. That's why I got traded. It wasn't because I wanted more money. Everybody wants more money.

I was back home in St. Louis after the season in 1967 and not feeling great. I had recently had exploratory back surgery and was healing. I received a call early in the morning from Bob Howsam. "Good morning," he said. I thought he was calling to check up on how I was doing, because I was hurt during the year. Before he could even say anything more, I said, "Mr. Howsam, it's so good to hear from you. Thank you for calling and checking up on me. I appreciate the call very much. I'm feeling much better than I was a few weeks ago."

And he said, "Well, I'm glad you're feeling good, because we just traded you this morning." I had spent eight years in professional baseball with the Reds. The first time you get traded, it's a shock—I don't care what anybody says.

Cincinnati had a pretty good team—a prelude to the Big Red Machine. After it sank in for a minute, my first question was, "Where was I traded to?"

"You've been traded to New York," Howsam answered. I was thinking that I was going to the Yankees. I followed them as a kid growing up; they had all those great players, and it seemed like they were in the World Series almost every year since I first started following baseball. Then I thought about Yankee Stadium—I could break a bat and hit it out of there in right field. And so I asked, "Who from the Yankees is going to be calling me?"

Howsam paused and said, "Um, it's not the Yankees."

I thought, *Oh, no.*

"It's the Mets," he said.

Now, back in those days, if you didn't beat the Mets two out of three games, that was a bad series. I wasn't crazy about New York for a couple of reasons, and the Mets were a bad team. I was hesitant to say anything more on the phone, or even to ask who I was traded for. (Turned out it was an infielder, Bob Johnson, who got traded again a couple months into the season.)

Howsam had traded lots of young players; he knew I was in shock. And yes, I *was* in shock! He then said, "This could be good for you. The general manager says he knows you." Growing up in St. Louis, I met Bing Devine, then the Cardinals' GM, at a tryout camp. I was 14, 15 years old. Devine came up to me and told me I was too young to be there and asked to see my birth certificate. He kept tabs on me, though I wound up signing with the Reds. Before Major League Baseball inaugurated a draft in 1965, a teenager could sign with whoever he liked—or usually whoever offered the most money. Or any money at all.

About an hour after I talked to Howsam about being traded to the Mets, Bing Devine called. He told me that he remembered me as a kid and scouted me with the Reds. He said, "The Mets are a great organization. You're going to love playing here, and we need some left-handed power." He said all the things you want to hear when you've been traded to a new team.

After he spoke I was a little relieved, and I told him, "Thanks for calling me. You made me feel a lot better."

He said I should come to New York and have the doctors check me out. He knew I had a bad back. We talked a little more, and he said he'd call again in a day or so. He didn't. A couple days later, I picked up the St. Louis paper, and it said something like, "Bing's Back." He had left the Mets to come back to the Cardinals as general manager. St. Louis had just won the World Series; the Mets had just finished 10th.

So in effect, I was his last trade as Mets GM. He just up and left after telling me what a great organization the Mets were and how he couldn't wait to see me. Now it was a double shock. Bing Devine was the one person I knew in the Mets organization, or at least he knew me. In reality I knew a few of the players but not many. I had played against Eddie Kranepool and a few others in the minors, but I really didn't know any of them well.

That was my welcome to New York. But in retrospect, the trade turned out to be the best thing for my baseball career. Two years later we won the World Series and my life changed forever. Coincidentally, we clinched the division title against the Cardinals, Bing Devine's club.

New Kid in Town

As I mentioned, I had never met or barely had interaction with about 99 percent of the Mets before I got there for spring training in 1968. One of the few guys I did know was Jerry Buchek, an infielder. Like me, he was from St. Louis, and was signed by the Cardinals the same year the Reds signed me (1959), and debuted in the major leagues at 19. Jerry was traded to the Mets in 1967. He was part of a group of major leaguers who went to a workout class at St. Louis University in the winter. It was Jerry, Mike Shannon, Bill White, Roy Sievers, me, and others. Besides Jerry, I didn't know much about anyone else when I got to St. Petersburg for spring training. I was one of the new kids on the block. There were a number of us who came over around the same time.

Tommie Agee, Al Weis, and J. C. Martin also came over that winter. Though they arrived in a couple of trades with the White Sox, we were all first-time Mets in spring training in 1968. It took me a few days to introduce myself to the people I didn't know. Of course, we all became best of friends after that.

But Tommie, Al, J. C., and I weren't the only new guys. Don't forget, the manager and most of the coaches were all new as well.

Inaugural Address

Gil Hodges's first year managing the Mets was 1968. Gil's wife, Joan, was from Brooklyn, and Gil lived there even when he was playing in Los Angeles and managing in Washington, so no doubt he was excited to be back home. Growing up in St. Louis, I was a Cardinals fan, but Gil was a part of those great Brooklyn Dodgers teams from the late 1940s through most of the '50s. The Dodgers played the Yankees every time they reached the World Series, and it did not go well. Those Yankees teams were so dominant. Those the Dodgers-Yankees World Series seemed to go six or seven games every time. The teams played six times in a 10-year span, and the lone win by the Dodgers was in 1955. Gil drove in the only two runs in Game 7 as Brooklyn finally won.

I don't remember meeting Gil when I came to New York after the trade to be checked out medically. And I don't recall meeting him at the couple of banquets in New York that I went to during that time. My first real meeting with Gil—and the team—was when I arrived at spring training in 1968.

Having been in the National League for three seasons, the impression I had of the Mets organization was anything but favorable. In St. Petersburg, I recollect thinking, *Here I am on a team that's known as the Lovable Losers—a team that lost 100 games almost every year, including 1967. The GM who traded for me, Bing Devine—one of the few people I knew in the organization—is gone. He went back to St. Louis, and that was after he told me what a great organization the Mets are.*

That first day of spring training—I think it was before we even ran a lap around the field—Gil gathered everyone together. It must have been 40 or so guys; the whole winter roster was there. Gil was right in front of us, and I only knew him from watching him as a kid growing up. I knew him by reputation as a tough but fair person. He wasn't a really tall guy, but he was well-built.

Gil started out by saying something like: "I want to welcome everyone here, and I just want to let you know that from now on, you will not be the same-old Mets." My first reaction was that even though I hadn't been there before, one thing I knew right off the bat was that this guy was serious. You could see he was a no-nonsense guy after one sentence.

From that moment on, I think the New York Mets changed as an organization. For their first six seasons, you could call the Mets inept and even a joke. They really were the laughingstock of baseball. From that first sentence of Gil's, I knew it was not going to be the same. The players who had been there before and the new guys alike realized it was a new era—the beginning of a different, more serious management.

Looking back to 1968, even though we weren't a great team that year, you could see that Gil's philosophy was very simple: you act right, you play right, and you find ways to win, whether it's 10–9, 7–6, 3–2, or 1–0. There would be a lot of 1–0 games that year.

That was the beginning of what I would say was an arm's-length relationship between Gil and me. I would go on to have a tremendous amount of respect for the man who was not only a great player but also a war hero. But I was not alone: he immediately had the respect of everyone on the team—young and old.

My Money's in My Other Uniform

The Reds trained in Tampa, so going to St. Petersburg for spring training wasn't a big change location-wise. Yet it was quite different in other ways. When I arrived at spring training in 1968, the Mets practiced at Huggins-Stengel Field (formerly Miller Huggins Field) as the Yankees had done years before, and we played our spring training games at Al Lang Stadium, which was the same ballpark the Cardinals used for games.

Huggins-Stengel Field was not a grandiose facility, but the setting was beautiful, with trees, palms, and a lake. It was a famous place where Babe Ruth, Lou Gehrig, Joe DiMaggio, and countless Hall of Famers spent spring training—including the managers it was named after: 1920s Yankees manager Miller Huggins and longtime Yankees manager—and first Mets manager—Casey Stengel.

The field jutted out in right field with a wire fence. And there was an extra infield for practice. The stands were set up like a small high school field. Bleachers were on the right-hand side near our clubhouse. Huggins-Stengel Field was fine for scrimmages or B games, which started around 10:00. For the B games they'd get 25 to 30 fans. There was nobody taking tickets. You could hear every sound made by the people who *were* there, and some fans were always eager to yell out some stuff.

There were only two fields at Huggins-Stengel Field: one was a game field, and the other was just an infield. And they had a little sliding pit where you would practice sliding and the coaches held infield practice, pitchers covering first, and drills like that.

That was it. I don't think there was a batting cage. We would run around the field one time in the morning, five minutes of calisthenics, and we were ready to go. The fence was pretty far. I can't guarantee that Babe Ruth didn't hit one out of the facility and into the water, but I never did—nor did I see anyone else do it.

Because the Cardinals practiced at Al Lang Stadium, it was convenient to have many of our spring training games against them. The stadium was a couple of miles away from Huggins-Stengel Field, and we would take cabs to get there for the game and then again to get back afterward. That was always interesting when five guys piled into a taxi. In uniform! Even when we were the home team and the Cardinals were on the road, we'd still have to ride back in the cabs in uniform as opposed to changing there. We'd get back in the cabs and be sweaty from playing and have dirt in our shoes from sliding. Following one long game, I got into the cab and—still in uniform—said to the cab driver, "I want to forget about this game. How much to take us to Miami?"

Of course the cabbie didn't drive us to the other side of the state that day. I wouldn't have had any money left after the cab fare and the manager's fine for going to the bars in uniform—and spikes. But I was tempted.

Icebreaker with Tom Seaver

The first time I faced Tom Seaver was in June 1967 at Shea Stadium. I was still with the Reds, and Seaver had a shutout going and the Mets had a 7–0 lead when I came up to pinch-hit in the ninth. I hit a three-run home run off him. He retired the last two Reds, and the Mets won 7–3. Seaver wound up National League Rookie of the Year and polished off the American League in the 15th inning to close out the All-Star Game in Anaheim. He pitched a lot of innings, didn't give up many home runs, and won a bunch of games for a team that lost north of 100 games in 1967.

When I got over to spring training with the Mets the following year, I didn't really know anybody. I'm basically a pretty shy person, and it wasn't easy introducing myself to the guys in the locker room. I finally decided to talk to Tom, who'd been the only bright spot on a bad Mets team the year before.

"Tom, hi. I'm Art—." He stopped me before I said my last name.

"I know who you are," he said.

"Really?" I asked.

"Yeah," he said. "And I remember that day in June when I was pitching that shutout in the ninth and you hit the three-run home run."

I didn't have much to say just then, and Tom kept talking. "I'll tell you what," he said. "We'll talk about it today, but how about we won't talk about it again?"

"Fair enough," I said.

We never talked about it again, and we became very good friends.

Since I'm bringing it up now, though, I'll say this: I looked up Seaver's starts as a rookie in 1967. The June 13 game would have been his first career shutout if I hadn't gone and spoiled it. (Sorry, not sorry.) Seaver got his first complete-game shutout a couple months later. He wound up with 61 shutouts in his career. That's an astounding number, and one more shutout by Tom would have broken a tie for seventh on the all-time list with another of my Mets teammates: Nolan Ryan.

The Grote Effect

Who's your catcher? That is one of the key questions for any team in any era. The answer usually determines how good a team is or how good it could be. Fans remember the catchers who are good hitters, but a catcher who is in control behind the plate is invaluable—no matter his batting average or his temper.

The first thing I have to say about Jerry Grote is that he was the best defensive catcher I ever saw. There was not one aspect of the game that he didn't do well: handling pitchers, pop flies, balls topped in front of the plate, runners trying to slide past him, and throwing out runners trying to steal. All of it. He was the best.

With that being said, I always believed that once the ballpark came into view, whether it was home or on the road, Jerry's demeanor and personality changed. He became very hardnosed and tough as nails. At night going out with a group of guys, he was fine, but once the ballpark came into view, it just did something to him—amped up his aggression. Maybe that's what made him so competitive.

He used to fire the ball back to the pitcher when he was angry. If you threw the ball in the dirt and maybe it hit him or bruised him or something, he'd fire that ball right back. And after the pitcher's delivery, he might be off the hill. So now he was a few feet closer to home plate, and Jerry would fire it. If a pitcher wasn't ready, look out! (Seaver and Koosman excepted.)

A lot of opposing players didn't like him, which seemed fine by Jerry. In a running battle of heavyweight competitors, Jerry and Lou Brock of the Cardinals used to yell at each other all the time. Lou was the dominant base-stealer of the day and an excellent hitter. Jerry saw his job as shutting him down. Brock told an interviewer that Grote "was the toughest catcher in the league to steal on."

Jerry turned out to be a pretty good hitter—a clutch hitter. There's no question that his defensive skills were excellent. Jerry started the All-Star Game in 1968, which was Johnny Bench's rookie year with the Reds. Bench started just about every other All-Star Game and dominated the Gold Glove after that. But Bench once said, "[If Jerry and I had been teammates], I would have been the third baseman and Grote would have been the catcher." Unfortunately, Jerry passed away recently, but his defensive abilities will always be remembered.

Car Gets Benched

Johnny Bench was a phenomenal catcher, but I have questions about his driving. He had a little fender bender with my car—a used Cadillac, emphasis on *used*—after he'd been called up to the majors by the Reds in August 1967. Bench took out my sister-in-law and took my car out as well. There wasn't much damage, and I'm not exactly sure if he was driving or if she was behind the wheel when they had the little accident. Whoever's fault it was, I never let him forget it.

Unlike at first base, where you can only talk to the first baseman after a single or a walk, every time you come up to bat, you are guaranteed to be next to the catcher—especially an All-Star like Bench, who started 130 times a year and almost never came out. Every time the Mets played the Reds, I'd come up to the plate and tell him, "You still owe me some money for my car."

J. C. and Stan the Man

When I arrived in St. Petersburg, I had never met about 99 percent of the Mets. There were three Jerrys on the team: Grote, Koosman, and Buchek. And I soon got to know catcher J. C. Martin.

You'd think that with Jerry Grote behind the plate, it wouldn't really matter who his backup was. But catcher is probably the most important defensive position in baseball. Besides being involved in every pitch, there's calling the game, handling signs, and being the last line of defense against players trying to score. It is a demanding position, and even the best catchers in the game take off 30 or more starts to avoid being completely worn out by September. Having a good second-string catcher is crucial—especially for a team with a first-class young pitching staff.

Gil Hodges knew it was important. The same day that the November 27, 1967, transaction went through to bring him from the Washington Senators (in a rare player-for-manager trade, Bill Denehy and $100,000 went to Washington in return for the beloved former Brooklyn Dodger), the Mets announced that J. C. Martin had been acquired from the White Sox. He was the player to be named later in a July deal that sent Ken Boyer to Chicago.

J. C. was a veteran left-handed-hitting catcher who could give our young pitchers a steady hand regardless of whether he or Grote were behind the plate. Gil had a say in another deal with the White Sox that fall, insisting the Mets get Tommie Agee and Al Weis, even though it cost New York Tommy Davis and two other young players as well as veteran pitcher Jack Fisher. The White Sox had been in the 1967 American League race up until the final week of the season; the Red Sox won the pennant on the last day. Having players who had experienced a pennant race was something that didn't hurt a team as raw as the Mets. Gil had been in the American League as a manager since 1963. He had firsthand knowledge of these guys, and I think that was a big part in suggesting they trade for them.

J. C. told me a story about when he was a young player and he hit a hard single to left field in a spring training game against St. Louis. He was on first base, and perennial All-Star Stan Musial started talking to him. Musial, holding J. C. on first, said to him, "It feels pretty good pulling a ball to right for a hit, doesn't it?"

"Sure does," J. C. said, but all he was thinking was, *I can't believe Stan the Man is talking to me.* He was a household name, a three-time MVP, a seven-time batting champion, and an All-Star for almost as many years as J. C. had been alive at that point.

"You know," Musial went on, "I noticed that it feels just as good when you get a hit to left field too."

J. C. said that his approach changed from that encounter. He looked to put the ball in play more instead of trying to pull every pitch. That's when singles and doubles were really at a premium, as pitching dominated the game more and more in the 1960s. J. C. wasn't a home-run hitter, and he never tried to be. He was in the major leagues for 14 years and won a World Series with us. Stan the Man, my hero, gave J. C. some great advice!

Al Weis

When Al Weis was traded to the New York Mets, he had the same reaction that I did: disappointment. Anyone traded to the Mets in the early and mid-1960s had that reaction. And if you were going from a contending ballclub to New York's "other team," it felt worse. Even Gil Hodges was surprised when he found out the Mets were looking to trade for him to manage the club. In his case, at least—along with New York–born coaches Eddie Yost and Joe Pignatano—he was going home. For North Carolinian Rube Walker, who had helped build an up-and-coming pitching staff in Washington, home was where Gil was. Like everyone who wound up at Shea Stadium in the late 1960s, being part of that New York Mets team would shape everything we did afterward. But that didn't make the impact upon arrival any less jarring.

Al Weis had missed most of the second half of 1967 with the White Sox. He was injured on a slide from Orioles star Frank Robinson that tore up his leg. He returned to the roster at the end of the season but did not play. He didn't play from June 1967 until he joined the Mets the following April.

Then came the trade that sent Al and Tommie Agee to New York. The Mets got him from the White Sox off a bad year—a year when he was hurt—and Al wound up one of the most unlikely World Series heroes ever.

He had no relationship with Gil Hodges before the trade, but Al later told me that coach Joe Pignatano passed along word that Hodges would not have made the trade for Tommie without Al being part of the deal. In hindsight, Al believes that the Mets got him because they had a number of young players who had military commitments due to the Vietnam War. Since some players were required to go away for weekend duty or weeks-long training—as happened with Bud Harrelson—the Mets looked at Al as someone who could take over at second base and shortstop.

I can tell you firsthand that Gil Hodges could impact your life even if you had few personal interactions with him. Al *never* had a one-to-one conversation with Hodges, but he said that he is forever eternally grateful for the chance Gil gave him to play as much as he did as a Met. As with most of our teammates, the Mets and the 1969 World Series in particular changed Al's life. He feels that being traded to the Mets was the best thing that happened to him in baseball. He still receives fan mail all the time from people who consider him a World Series hero on the 1969 championship team. Coincidently, his birthday, April 2, falls on the same day Gil Hodges died in 1972.

Filling in for Bud Harrelson during his military commit-ment became more than a part-time job for Al Weis. He started more games at shortstop than at second base in both 1968 and '69. Al also decided that there were enough left-hitting infielders in the Mets organization, so in 1969 he stopped switch-hitting and just batted right for the rest of his career. Dropping the side of the plate where he hit .206 proved a wise decision for Al, but it required some adjustment. He hit just .172 in 1968, but in 1969 he was as fierce a .215 hitter as you'll ever see.

His two regular-season home runs that year came on back-to-back days in July during our battle with the first-place Cubs at Wrigley Field. Overall, Al hit a stunning .309 with runners in scoring position during the 1969 season. Ask the Orioles how tough a hitter Al Weis could be.

Along the Coaching Lines

The whole coaching staff was great. It really had a Brooklyn flair to it. Everyone had some New York background. Rube Walker was Southern, but he played for the Brooklyn Dodgers. Joe Pignatano was from Brooklyn, and he debuted with the Dodgers during their last year in Brooklyn. Piggy was also with the Mets their first year in New York—in his last at-bat in the majors, he hit into a triple play in the last game of the year for the 1962 Mets. Eddie Yost never played in New York, but he was from there. Eddie was born in Brooklyn and grew up in Queens. He went to NYU and then went into the military in World War II. And Yogi, who ferried soldiers to the Normandy beaches on D-Day, was from St. Louis like me. Yet as the catcher on Casey Stengel's great Yankees teams, Yogi was as synonymous with New York as any coach in baseball.

All the coaches were involved in the pregame, hitting fly balls or ground balls—those are nice memories, because teams today don't really even do infield practice. Once the game was over and we got back to the hotel on the road, I rarely saw our coaches. That was all right, because if they saw you somewhere you weren't supposed to be or out past curfew on the road, you wound up getting fined. The coaches were as loyal to Gil as if they'd been in his platoon when he was a marine at Okinawa.

Yogi

After I was traded to the Mets in November 1967, I spent the winter building up in my mind the St. Louis connection with Yogi Berra. I am one of about 300 guys from St. Louis who have made the majors over the years. Of that long list, the best player of them all was Yogi. He grew up in an Italian neighborhood called the Hill with another well-known catcher and personality: Joe Garagiola. Yogi won 10 World Series and three American League MVP Awards as an All-Star catcher for the Yankees, and he won another pennant with the Yankees in his one year as a manager before he wound up a coach on the Mets.

I'd never met Yogi, and when I got to the Mets, I was just in awe of him. In my mind I figured that since we were both from St. Louis, he was going to take me under his wing. Well, 10 or 12 days into spring training I don't think he had any idea who I was. I don't think he even knew my name, much less that we were from the same city.

In our first spring training game of 1968, I got a single, and Yogi was coaching first base. I rounded the bag and I came back to the base, and now I was face-to-face with Yogi, who had never said a word to me; it was finally an opportunity for him to acknowledge that I existed. It was early in the game, Bob Gibson was pitching for the Cardinals, I was on the bag, and I was thinking Yogi was going to say something to me. A first base coach has some responsibility: usually they remind you of the situation of the game, how many outs there are, or say something like, "The pitcher's got a good move" or maybe even, "Nice hit." So I was standing on the bag, and Yogi came over and grabbed the back of my pants. I thought he was going to say any of these things, or at least speak my name. He barked out, "Hey, you're on first base. Pay attention!" That was it.

Our relationship kind of developed after that but not so much in a teacher-pupil capacity. As time went on, I realized he really wasn't the hitting coach, because he never talked to us about hitting. One time I said to him, "Yogi, I'm really struggling. What should I do?" He said, "Well, see it and hit it." That was the extent of it. Once we got to know each other, we got to be pretty good friends. And he even remembered my name. Well, at least he called me Sham!

One night Yogi called up to our room to do a bed check to make sure we weren't breaking curfew. I don't remember Gil Hodges ever having another bed check in all my time with the Mets, but this one happened in Chicago in 1968. Since Wrigley Field had no lights, I guess Gil figured we were all out and wanted to make sure no one was staying out too late with a game the next afternoon. It would be another two decades or more before even the best-paid ballplayer carried around a portable phone, so the only way to reach us was via our room phones. I picked up the phone next to the bed. It was Yogi.

"Are you in?" Yogi asked.

"Of course I'm in," I said. And I reminded him, "Didn't I just answer the phone?"

He moved on to the next order of business. "What about your roommate?" Ken Boswell was out, but I wasn't giving up my roommate over the phone. I said, "He's sleeping. You want me to wake him up?"

Yogi said, "No. As long as you say he's in." That was the bed check! What's a little white lie between ballplayers from the same hometown?

Yost

I used to tell Eddie Yost, "You really look like a coach. The uniform fits you perfectly. You've got that perfect coach's look." He was a great coach, a student of the game.

Eddie was a great player. They called him the Walking Man because he was always leading the league in walks in the 1950s. Now they might not even want him in the majors because he didn't hit a lot of home runs. Guys like him who weren't big and weren't home-run hitters had to learn everything about the game to stay in baseball. Eddie wasn't going to get by with that 1-for-4 with a home run like a lot of power hitters. He'd go 1-for-3 with a double, a run scored, and two walks. And he played excellent defense at third base. Eddie played his first game in the majors at 17 years old for the old Washington Senators during World War II; when he was old enough, he went into the military.

He had to know the game to stay around so long, and that's how he got into coaching. He was a coach for 23 years. He was coaching in Washington before Gil got there. That's how they ended up together.

Rube

In my and my roommate Kenny Boswell's case, pitching coach Rube Walker was our liaison with Gil. Rube was a wonderful guy. He was a big old southerner, and he knew everything about his staff. Though his main concern was the pitchers, he kept an eye out on everything for Gil Hodges. Unlike a lot of pitching coaches, he had been a catcher, not a pitcher. He understood the uncertain combination of pain and the enthusiasm that made up the life of an everyday ballplayer. He batted .227 for his career, so he knew what it took to stay on a major league roster. He backed up the great Roy Campanella most of his years in Brooklyn, which is where he got to know Gil so well.

He was always next to Gil. Rube was the guy that if you had something to talk about, a problem with anything, you went to him. Fortunately, we never really had many problems. I don't know if an outfielder would even talk to a pitching coach now. There's no infield practice, and everyone has their specialized area. The only time a first baseman would have much interaction with a pitching coach now is if they were all standing around on the mound during a visit to talk to the pitcher.

Rube was so respected that he served as a pitching coach for 20 consecutive seasons—with the Washington Senators, Mets, and Braves. He was the pitching coach for the Mets from 1968 to 1981 under five different managers: Gil Hodges, Yogi Berra, Roy McMillan, Joe Frazier, and Joe Torre.

Rube would go down and smoke near the runway behind the bathroom in the dugout. So would Gil and Yogi—and quite a few ballplayers too. On his way back to sitting by Gil—his usual seat—he'd always stop and tell Kenny Boswell and me (we usually sat together on the other end of the bench), "You guys are really exciting ballplayers." We would just smile.

Piggy

Joe Pignatano was the king of the bullpen. Though I was in right field and as close as any player on the field to Piggy's domain in the home bullpen at Shea, I didn't have a lot of interaction with him. Obviously I dealt with Eddie Yost, who was the third base coach; Yogi Berra, the first base coach; and Rube Walker, the pitching coach, who served as Gil's lieutenant.

Of all the coaches, Joe was the most outspoken. He would get involved in the locker room banter, whereas the others really didn't.

Joe had another life in right field: gardening. Piggy was very conscientious about the garden. As his reputation grew, the word around the clubhouse and the league was that he had become a farmer out there in the right-field bullpen. I never got one of his tomatoes. I was a meat-and-potatoes guy back then.

Every team has characters in the bullpen, but he had the benefit of some real special personalities out there: Tug McGraw, Ron Taylor, and Don Cardwell. Joe was very protective of that group. A relationship between Joe and someone in that bullpen was much greater than one with me or a position player or someone on the bench. That was par for the course.

My Dad, Long-Distance Hitting Coach

The Mets didn't believe in hitting coaches, but I already had one in my family. When I was playing a game and my father was there, he would typically arrive when the gates opened. He wanted to see batting practice, look at my swing. He was the kind of father who, when I'd have two hits in a game—and this goes back to Little League and high school—he'd say, "That's great; you had two hits. But what happened the other two times you batted?" He was a little overpowering in that regard.

One day after I came over to the Mets, we were playing the Reds at Shea, and I saw Tommy Helms before the game. He was my teammate in Cincinnati and a very good second baseman who was the 1966 Rookie of the Year and an All-Star. We said hello to each other from a bit of a distance, thanks to the fraternization rules. Tommy told me the Reds had just come from St. Louis and he brought greetings.

"I saw your dad the other day in St. Louis," Tommy yelled over to me. We came up together through the Reds system, and whenever the team went to St. Louis, Tommy and a couple of other players would go to my house and have dinner. "Did my dad ask you for tickets?"

"No," Tommy said. "He wanted to know if I knew why you'd gone 0-for-4 the other night." Tommy just smiled. I couldn't help but smile too. Then *I* wondered why I had gone 0-for-4 the other night.

The Fungo Rifle

I was really happy Gil Hodges had enough confidence to put me at first base, because he was a great defensive first baseman. He won the first Gold Glove by a first baseman—and the first three Rawlings gave—in the 1950s, when only one award was given for both leagues. It was Gil's idea to make me into a first baseman, and he tutored me himself.

Gil hit me ground balls before games, especially in spring training. I'm not kidding—he would try to kill me. He would hit the ball with a fungo bat as hard as he could hit them. If the ball came up and hit you, so be it. One of my most vivid memories was him hitting me ground balls that were sizzling. I always made sure I was wearing a cup. In the long run, it was good for me; in the short term, I probably wished someone else was hitting me fungoes. The other coaches—Yogi Berra, Joe Pignatano, Eddie Yost—would hit some ground balls that were not too difficult to play. Gil would not let you off the hook. That was not his way. When he had that fungo bat, you'd better have your head up and have that cup in the right place.

If a ball came up and drilled me in the shin or the ankle, he would crack, "That didn't hurt, did it?" I would never give him the satisfaction of saying it hurt, though it did.

After I left the Mets, I heard that he hit bullet fungoes to new acquisition Jim Fregosi, an All-Star shortstop Gil wanted to work at becoming a third baseman. Jim and I ended up being good friends after we both retired. Back in 1972, though, Jim didn't know that Gil took it upon himself to make him into a corner infielder. A laser shot by Gil injured Fregosi's throwing hand and put him in a cast. Why am I not surprised? Gil liked to put a hurt on you when he picked up that fungo bat. It was his way of telling you to get ready.

That story about Fregosi makes me feel even better that I was able to survive Gil's ground balls unscathed. If I could endure what he dished out with the fungo bat, I could handle whatever was hit my way in a game.

Even though I didn't have a really close relationship with Gil, in many ways I think he helped shape many things in me—things I still think about and use all the time.

Chapter 2

1968: PRE-MIRACLE

A Strange Beginning

We started the 1968 season on the road in California. In Cincinnati I was used to opening the season at home, which remained a tradition in the MLB for many years. It was usually a freezing but festive Monday afternoon at Crosley Field. Now I was a Met, and we were out West. When we left camp in St. Petersburg, we first went to Phoenix and Anaheim for a few exhibition games, and then to Palm Springs for Easter weekend. I thought it was a great trip already. Then we opened the season in San Francisco.

Sadly, Martin Luther King Jr. was assassinated in Memphis on April 4, 1968. Before I ever played a regular-season game as a Met—or Gil Hodges managed a game for the team—all the clubs held a vote and decided not to play the day of Martin Luther King's burial: Tuesday, April 9, 1968. That resulted in us playing just one game in San Francisco, on April 10; then we played twice in Los Angeles and two more in Houston before finally returning to New York for our home opener.

We lost the season opener at Candlestick—my Mets debut—in the ninth. I had two hits against Juan Marichal, playing left field. In a sign of things to come in what people wound up calling the Year of the Pitcher, our next five games were all shutouts (and not all in our favor). Jerry Koosman, a rookie breaking camp with the Mets, threw two of them, one in Los Angeles and the other in our home opener at Shea. In the last four games of our season-opening road trip, we won two games by scores of 4–0 and lost two by scores of 1–0. That second 1–0 loss, in Houston, lasted almost as many innings as three games combined.

I started the game at the Astrodome and went 2-for-4 against Don Wilson, who threw really hard. In the ninth inning, Gil took me out for a pinch-runner—Cleon Jones—and he ended up batting six times!

I remember Tommie Agee, already off to a tough start after Bob Gibson hit him in the head in our very first spring training game, went 0-for-10 in that marathon Houston game. He came into the game hitting more than .300 to start his Mets career, but he did not get another hit until May. We'll never be sure if Gibson's pitch to the head was a message that said, "Welcome to the National League." Whatever the intent, Agee did not get a warm welcome in the National League. He started an 0-for-34 slump that night; his average never recovered in what was a tough year.

Ron Swoboda also went 0-for-10 that night. The first four batters in our lineup went 2-for-39 with one walk in the game. Jerry Grote caught all 24 innings. Our staff threw all those zeroes on the scoreboard only to lose on a bad hop grounder that went for an error on Al Weis to end the game.

The infield hadn't been raked in almost 20 innings. A few players complained to our player rep, Ed Kranepool, that the field should be dragged every five innings no matter how long the game went. We lost the game, but we got the rule changed. If that bad-hop grounder hadn't happened, with the Astrodome's bad lighting and background, that game might still be going on!

Koosman Comes Out Firing

Jerry Koosman, who'd only pitched a handful of games in the majors and had never won a game before 1968—pitched a shutout in his first two starts of the year. Kooz, as we called him (sometimes Koo), won four times in April.

His start in the home opener against San Francisco on April 17 showed everyone the kind of pitcher he could be—and *would* be. The first three Giants reached base in the top of the first inning at Shea; Willie Mays, Jim Ray Hart, and catcher Jack Hiatt were to follow. Koosman mowed right through them, striking out Mays and Hiatt and getting Hart to foul out. He allowed no one else to get to third base the rest of the game.

That 3–0 win was also the first time New York fans got to see their beloved Gil Hodges—hero of the Brooklyn faithful— manage the home club in Flushing. Though it was surely of less concern to New Yorkers, that afternoon was also my first game on the home field side at Shea Stadium—and my first start at first base since 1965.

Pitching out of the first inning against a tough San Francisco lineup in front of a packed house was a pretty good indication of how tough Kooz was as a competitor. He was not only a cool character but he was quiet—for a while, anyway.

I still talk to Jerry frequently, and I told him not long ago that I didn't remember him being a cutup or outspoken in 1968 like he was later on. "I wasn't," he said. "We had Tug and we had Swoboda as the main characters on the team. I was really kind of shy and didn't get involved in some of the craziness from the guys who had been around." Jerry watched what was happening as a rookie, even as he was setting franchise records. By the next year, though, Kooz had segued into the McGraw territory.

They didn't call 1968 the Year of the Pitcher for nothing. The National League ERA was below 3.00, and the Mets stood fourth at 2.72. Mets pitchers put together 25 shutouts, second in the NL. That was a good thing, because we were blanked 22 times and scored the second-fewest runs in the league (2.91 runs per game). If a Mets starter gave up more than two runs, odds were they'd take the loss. The Mets' left-right aces figured out the math: Koosman had a 2.08 ERA, and Seaver's was 2.20. Though that was still a long way from Bob Gibson's microscopic 1.12 ERA, the lowest in the National League since 1906.

Though the Mets finished ninth in a 10-team league in 1968, a 23-year-old right-hander and a 25-year-old lefty were both All-Stars—with Koosman fanning 1967 Triple Crown winner Carl Yastrzemski of the Red Sox for the last out. The Mets had more arms on the way, and a manager who was drumming the losing mentality out of his men. People with their eyes open were starting to take notice of what was happening at Shea, even if most clubs still dismissed the team as a joke.

Even Some Batting Practice Pitchers Were Legends in 1968

At home we faced batting practice pitchers hired by the team. That was another thing Joe Pignatano would do—figure out who would come pitch BP at Shea. On the road, we had coaches or players who weren't starting the game doing the pitching in batting practice. Very few teams had batting practice pitchers who would travel. If you were lucky, someone a coach or a player knew might come in and pitch BP for an afternoon. The rest of the time, it was usually Yogi throwing BP. We made do. That's the way it was. You weren't facing the kind of pitcher you'd see in a game. It was practice. If you didn't adjust for the game and the opposing pitcher, you were overmatched. It was that simple!

One time after I finished in the batting cage, I yelled out to Yogi, "That's the worst batting practice pitching I've ever seen!"

"Well," Yogi hollered back, "go complain to a coach!" I guess he forgot he was a coach!

At home the Mets paid some guys to pitch BP. (For example, my friend and future co-owner in a restaurant with me, Tony Ferrara, later pitched BP for both the Mets and Yankees during the 1980s and 1990s.) During the 1960s, batting practice pitchers were either former players or those who were simply decent athletes.

On the road, you went with anyone who was available. That often meant Gil Hodges or Yogi Berra. Gil would throw from close to the mound—and like most things, he took the task seriously. Yogi would move the cage up to about 35 feet away and throw from there. Joe Pignatano might be from a few feet farther back. Very rarely did pitchers throw batting practice to you during the season. I did my share of BP pitching, usually on days when I wasn't starting. One thing it did was give me a chance to work out my frustration about sitting on the bench. I also thought it strengthened my arm a bit and was a good workout. They'd send you out with a time limit—usually 10 to 12 minutes so you didn't throw out your arm.

Something people don't understand is that in batting practice, you're not facing pitchers who have the kind of stuff you'd get in a game from Bob Gibson, Juan Marichal, Sandy Koufax,

Don Drysdale, or any of the great pitchers of that era. Nobody was throwing batting practice with that kind of velocity or movement. But there were exceptions, and sometimes you actually had people whose job it was to pitch batting practice. You had to watch what you wished for.

Nolan Ryan. There may not be a pitcher in history who was worse to hit against in BP than Nolan. Especially when he was young, wild, and out of practice. Nolan was in the army reserve in 1968–69, and he was often away on weekends in his native Texas. When he came back to New York during the week, the Mets would try to get him some work and have him pitch batting practice. Still just 21 in 1968, and not yet a full-time member of the rotation, he wanted to impress the coaches. In batting practice he wasn't throwing strikes, but he certainly was throwing hard.

It was a waste of time trying to stand in and hit against him in batting practice. Nolan wasn't about to just lob it in; he wanted to get some work in. And the coaches wanted to see him throw. Most of the time Nolan threw BP, it was against the extra men, not the regulars. Good luck to them!

I didn't envy those guys bearing the brunt of a rusty Ryan. He was out of form from having to spend his weekends with the army reserve in Texas, flying to New York to get in playing shape with the team, and then going back to Texas the next weekend. He had been doing this for the better part of a year in the minors when I got to New York in 1968, and he spent much of '69 shuttling back and forth to base.

When he was young, Nolan was especially tough to play behind. He was 3–2 on a lot of batters. And when he threw strikes, batters had a hard time handling it and fouled off a lot of pitches. There were long at-bats, long innings, and long games. I'm sure someone doing Sabermetrics could come up with a factor or formula for pitchers who threw strikes, such as Greg Maddux and Tom Seaver, and compare it with the errors committed and unearned runs allowed when playing behind someone constantly walking batters or going 3–2 all the time. You just were never on your toes in the field with the pitchers who didn't throw strikes consistently. When you're in the field, you expect to get the ball, but standing out there longer doesn't make you sharper on defense. There's a saying I've heard from the JUGS Gun world of scouting that we live in now, but it applies to any era: "I don't care how fast you throw ball four."

No Batting Coach, No Batting Gloves

When you're standing at the plate, put the trademark on the bat straight up. That's what I was taught, but not by a major league coach. It took me a number of years as a professional to understand that hitting the ball hard and making the opposition field the ball helps your team win. It's a simple philosophy: batted balls fall in, grounders can find holes, fielders boot balls or make bad throws. On a strikeout, the only fielding the opposition does is tossing the ball around on its way back to the pitcher.

None of the teams I was on had a coach to talk to us about hitting. There was no facility under the stands in which to take batting practice on rainy days or during games. Whatever extra practice we got was with the help of coaches who were willing to throw—and you had to find a coach able to put in the time. No coach ever grabbed me and said, "Why don't you try this or that at the plate? It might work."

The Mets had coaches help with infield and outfield play, but no coach ever talked to me about hitting. The Mets may have listed Yogi Berra as the hitting coach on paper, but that would have been news to him. He was an all-time great, but he wasn't an orthodox hitter, and it might have been difficult for him to explain the basics of hitting. He was just a free-swinging guy who made contact and had power.

At least I had Frank Robinson to offer hitting advice early in my career. He was the MVP and star of the Reds and gave me good advice when I first came up to the majors in 1965. Frank told me to work on hitting the ball to the opposite field, even against batting practice pitchers. That helped me concentrate and get into good habits. It's a good thing I listened to Frank when I had the chance, because he was traded to Baltimore after my rookie season.

As I got older and became a better hitter, I felt the key to success was to do in games what I did in practice. It's very hard to talk to kids about that now, because their perception of the game is taking these wild swings and hitting it out of the ballpark in batting practice and in games. I don't think you're helping your team or your career by doing that.

Few people even used batting gloves when I played. I used one on my left hand because I had had two operations on my hand before I even made it to the majors. My second operation occurred during my third season in the minor leagues in Macon, Georgia. It still affected me a lot when I got to the big leagues. But using a glove to protect the hand while batting was my interpretation of what I should do, not something anyone told me. What model batting glove did I use? None. There weren't any at the time. I used a golf glove.

Strikeouts

Everybody is different. I used to take strikeouts home with me. Even if I had a couple of hits in the game, a strikeout would still bother me because I thought striking out was the worst thing you could do. You give your team no chance; there's no percentage in it. Some players can walk away with no problem after it's over—even after a tough loss—but that wasn't me.

Fraternize at First

There were a lot more rules and regulations regarding what players could do on the field when I played. Hard as it may seem compared with today, the major leagues had fraternization rules. You could go 10 feet from the batting cage and say hello to somebody, but there was no one-on-one conversation with someone on another team. An umpire might be sitting in the stands watching it all. Players would occasionally be fined for fraternizing with players on opposing teams. The idea was to keep some appearance that guys in different uniforms were competitive rivals, so the major leagues tried to ensure opponents did not have relationships. I thought it was a good idea, but it doesn't mean I didn't take part in conversations with opposing players whom I knew when I had the chance.

There was an actual rule that fraternizing was a no-no. It's still in the rule book:

Rule 4.06 No Fraternization

Players in uniform shall not address or mingle with spectators, nor sit in the stands before, during, or after a game. No manager, coach or player shall address any spectator before or during a game.

Players of opposing teams shall not fraternize at any time while in uniform.

If you've been to a game an hour before it starts in the last 30 years, it's pretty obvious that the rule is not enforced. The last time anyone paid any attention to this rule was during COVID, when people could potentially pass on the illness.

Now it's back to being a hug-a-thon. But that wasn't the case in the late 1960s.

For me, there were so many players in the National League who I grew up watching. From the dream outfield at seemingly every All-Star Game—Hank Aaron, Willie Mays, and Roberto Clemente—to less popular but excellent players who would go on to the Hall of Fame, such as Billy Williams, Willie Stargell, and Willie McCovey. I idolized all these guys. I would study their swings in batting practice from the other dugout and then stand on the same field with them during the game. Just five or six years earlier, I had been watching them from the stands and on TV as I was growing up.

Cincinnati manager Dick Sisler had me play a game at first against the Mets. As a matter of fact, I didn't even have a first baseman's glove. Gil Hodges was the first manager who put me at first base and worked with me at it. That was great, because it not only gave me more opportunities to get in the lineup—or go in late in the game after double switches—but first base was one place you got to say anything you wanted to one of those stars without worrying about the strict fraternization rules.

In one game Hank Aaron got on first base, and there I was standing next to him; one of my idols had a foot on the same base as me. I was in awe, but I went through the motions of holding him on. Something was happening on the field, a mound visit from the catcher or a break in the action that gave me a little more time. I dared to speak—and took the liberty of calling him Hank. I said, "Hank, how does it feel coming to the ballpark knowing you're going to get two or three hits every day?"

It looked to me like he got hits every single day. He didn't, but he wound up with 3,771 career hits, so it sure felt like he was in the midst of a 3,000-game hitting streak. Against the Mets he batted .295 with 45 home runs in his career.

"I don't know if I'm going to get two or three hits today," Hank replied, "but if I don't get them today, I'm going to get them tomorrow." What that told me was that he was never worried about going 0-for-4 like some of us were. The fact that he even acknowledged me was unbelievable.

"Hank," I went on, "I really love to watch you hit. I love your swing."

He said to me, "I like your swing too."

That was one of the highlights of my life—Hank Aaron said he liked my swing.

The Draft

There were two drafts for which I was ineligible. The first was for the military. Men 18 and older were obligated to register for the military draft. This requirement was waived for me because of the two hand operations I had undergone. Plus I was married, which was taken into account for exemptions at that time. I could play baseball, but the military service was not interested in me.

The amateur baseball draft was put into place in 1965, six years after I was signed by the Reds after they scouted me that summer. The draft didn't do much to make salaries higher— that didn't really happen until the 1970s. Some say the draft was instituted to cut down the huge bonuses some big-name college players were getting. Whatever the motivation, it was better for young players—as was the creation of more teams in expansion to add more jobs at the big-league level. Before that, a lot of players just had to wait in the minors for that break that sometimes never came.

The amateur draft was a culmination of teams deciding to change the system in place, in which the rich got richer and the poor got poorer. The Yankees were the dominant ballclub in the American League for the better part of five decades until the mid-1960s. Their Double-A and Triple-A teams filled up with prospects, and those guys were used in trades to teams with no pipeline at all, such as the Kansas City A's (before Charlie Finley bought that franchise). The Yankees would send a bunch of young players they had no room for in the majors and bring back a budding star such as Roger Maris, Clete Boyer, or Ryne Duren.

My good friend Deron Johnson was a perfect example of someone getting buried in the minors because there was no room on the major league team. He hit 25 home runs every year for five years in their system (except his first season, when he hit 24), with a handful of at-bats at Yankee Stadium before he was sent to Kansas City. He ended up with the Reds, and we were teammates.

If it weren't for the amateur draft, who knows what would have happened to the Mets. After losing an astounding 340 games their first three seasons under the old system, the Mets couldn't go anywhere but up. They made some mistakes—such as drafting Steve Chilcott instead of Reggie Jackson with the first overall pick in 1966—but every team has blundered when it comes to not picking this guy or giving up on that guy. In the first draft in 1965, the Mets picked a high school pitcher named Nolan Ryan in the 12th round.

The Stand-In

You meet guys along the way who really are characters. Every team had them, and the Mets were no exception. The 1968 team had Tug McGraw, Ron Swoboda, and Jerry Koosman. Those guys stuck around because they had potential and delivered. Not everybody did.

Despite already having Jerry Grote and J. C. Martin, I thought the Mets were going to have three catchers in 1968. Gil Hodges decided that Greg Goossen would move from behind the plate to first base. He'd already moved me into a part-time first base spot with Ed Kranepool, and maybe Gil figured we needed a right-handed-hitting first baseman too.

Greg had a penchant for showing off—and not hitting much. The Mets drafted him from his hometown Los Angeles Dodgers in the first-year draft in 1965 and put him in the majors by September of that season. His first manager, Casey Stengel, wasn't overly impressed. There's a great story about Casey touting his young players to the press: "See that fellow over there, [Ed Kranepool]? He's 20 years old. In 10 years he has a chance to be a star. Now, that fellow over there, [Goossen], he's 19. In 10 years he has a chance to be 29." Greg would be long gone from the Mets by the time he reached that age.

One day Gil Hodges caught Goossen doing high dives off the diving board at the Shamrock Hotel in Houston. Greg got fined. He didn't play much after that, but he batted more than 100 times and hit just .208 in 1968. Even on the team with the lowest batting average in the National League, that was too low. He was traded to the expansion Seattle Pilots for Jim Gosger. Goossen had a bit more baseball fame as a recurring comedy figure in Seattle teammate Jim Bouton's revealing memoir *Ball Four*. Bouton called him "a flake" and described Goossen as "a burly guy with kinky blond hair who looks like a bouncer in an English pub." Greg worked with his brothers as a boxing trainer and cut enough of a figure to be an actor.

For years he was a stand-in for Gene Hackman, guaranteed a nice fee in any film the Oscar winner was in.

Read Shamsky in the *Post*

Writer Maury Allen talked me into doing an article every Saturday in the *New York Post* in 1968. The articles would comprise what was transpiring during the week, with some quips thrown in. Maury basically wrote them, and I checked them out. He did a great job, but I was shy and didn't want a lot of attention at the time. That was my first foray into writing. I decided to stop doing it because I didn't want any antagonism from the guys if I went into a slump, started not playing well, or got hurt. It ran for a few months in the *Post*.

Later on I wrote articles myself. Was I right all the time? Absolutely not. But the motivation for most pieces I wrote was to get people to think.

I wrote some articles for the *New York Times*. One of them in 1983 was about how to cut down on batters getting hit by pitches. Pitchers had free rein to do anything like that—hitting batters with no real consequences. I took the position that if a pitcher hit a batter and that batter was out for any substantial length of time, the pitcher should have to sit out too.

I was working as broadcaster at that point, and I ran into Don Drysdale, who was calling games for ABC. He complained to me that my solution penalized pitchers for a mistake. I told him, "If you have an independent doctor check out the batter who got hurt and if he had to miss a week with an injury, the pitcher should also lose a week. Why should fans of the team be deprived of their player while the pitcher that hit him just goes on pitching?" Drysdale, who led the National League in hit batsmen five times, agreed to disagree.

A reader wrote in to the *Times* about my article and suggested that pitchers might be more careful throwing inside if a batter got two bases when hit by a pitch. Interesting idea.

In *Kiner's Korner*

Kiner's Korner was a postgame (and sometimes pregame) interview TV show hosted by Mets broadcaster Ralph Kiner that aired on WOR-TV in New York City. The *Kiner's Korner* production room was right down the hall from our clubhouse at Shea. The production for *Kiner's Korner* was interesting. They got the whole set together in about five minutes. It was sort of my introduction to the behind-the-scenes workings of television. The room was small, and the walls were like cardboard. Conditions could be hazardous on the set. If the door opened and some wind whipped down the runway from the dugout, there was a chance the whole set might collapse in the middle of an interview.

Those folding walls with all the National League team names on them looked cool on TV. It wasn't a big area, and you had a couple of cameras there with you along with some behind-the-scenes people. A little 1960s set may sound small-time, but as a player talking with a star such as Ralph on TV in the media capital of New York, it sure felt like I'd hit it big.

Sinatrama

The team hotel in Philadelphia was the Bellevue-Stratford Hotel, where in 1976 bacteria in the air-conditioning system resulted in the deadly Legionnaires' disease following an American Legion convention. In 1968 we were just sick of sitting around the hotel, and we were aware of a unique watering hole not far away called Sinatrama that was solely dedicated to Frank Sinatra. (A year later I would run into the singer in person during our victory lap of Las Vegas in the fall of 1969.)

Kenny Boswell and I walked into this little alleyway not far from the hotel. To say it in Sinatra-ese, "This joint served the kind of hooch that Frank liked and played the kind of tunes that he dug: his own." The Chairman of the Board actually had nothing to do with the place and never visited, though his parents, from Hoboken, did stop by once.

Both Kenny and I liked Sinatra, but Ken really *loved* his music. Why a second baseman from the middle of Texas was so fired up about Sinatra cannot be explained. But Sinatrama was the place to go if you loved Ol' Blue Eyes, because that was all they played at the place. Every song on the jukebox was Sinatra—and if no one put any coins in the machine, it automatically played Sinatra anyway.

It was good and it was bad. It was good because I loved Sinatra, though not as much as Ken. If you had a good game, it was great to celebrate and belt out Sinatra tunes. But if you had a bad game, there were plenty of Sinatra songs that could make you even more depressed. And if you weren't playing at all, the slow Sinatra songs really got you down. The place had these fluorescent lights that showed all the lint on your jacket. Good thing Donn Clendenon wasn't around then to pick on us for what we were wearing and how much lint our ugly outfits collected.

I liked vodka, though I wasn't a big drinker. Ken drank Jack Daniel's. He told me the story that growing up in Austin his father drove a beer delivery truck for a Texas lager called Pearl beer, so all he ever drank growing up was Pearl beer. When the Mets chose him in the first major league draft in 1965 (fourth round out of Sam Houston State), Kenny signed with the team and was sent to Auburn, New York, for his first year in pro ball. He went to this bowling alley, Cayuga Lanes in Auburn, and saw the rows of liquor bottles behind the bar. So he decided, "Now that I'm in professional baseball, I'm going to drink what some of the idols I've read about drink." He ordered a Jack Daniel's and water. The bartender said to him, "Son, when you drink Jack Daniel's, you don't drink it with anything else; you drink it on the rocks."

That was the beginning of his big-league drink of choice. I learned a lot about my roommate that night we went to Sinatrama. Maybe one of us was celebrating a good game and the other was trying to forget a bad one. Sinatra's music went with both—like Jack on the rocks.

Trav_lers Motel (Always a Different Letter Out)

When I came to New York, I didn't really have a place to stay. Someone recommended the Travelers Motel. "Close to Shea," they said. "A number of other players are staying there," they said. It was right across the street from LaGuardia Airport. It's still there, though it's now aptly called the Landing at LaGuardia hotel.

Every time we went on the road, they let us check out so we didn't have to pay for rooms when we weren't there. They let us store whatever clothes we didn't take with us. That saved us money. The bulbs they bought for the sign must have been the cheap kind, because there was always one letter missing in *Travelers*. And whenever I came back from a road trip, a different letter was burned out.

In New York to Stay

I stayed at the Travelers Motel until June 1968. My wife and kids had stayed in St. Louis for the early part of the season because we had two young children—the eldest was in school—and they couldn't come to New York until classes got out. When they arrived, Mets traveling secretary Lou Niss—who seemed to know everybody in the city—put me in touch with people who lived in Forest Hills who had a house to rent. We rented that house from June until the season was over at the end of September. In other years, when the season was over, I just went back to my hometown, St. Louis, but when the 1968 season was over, we made plans to move to Manhattan.

When I arrived from the Reds, I didn't have a great impression of New York. I wasn't enamored by the city. It can take some getting used to, and then one day you can't imagine living anywhere else. I'd started to fall in love with everything about the city, including the fan base the Mets had. We hadn't won anything at all, but we knew if we could get something together as a team, the people were there to fall for us as hard as we'd fallen for them.

Our first apartment was in Midtown between First and Second Avenues, right near the Star Diner. A fella named Gus owned the diner, and I ate there a lot. Then we won the World Series the next year, and it was difficult going anywhere to eat. I have lived on the East Side of New York from that point on.

Down in Atlanta

It was the last week of the 1968 season, and I was playing first base in a late-September game against the Braves in Atlanta, so I didn't really have any idea something was wrong with Gil Hodges. Kenny Boswell and I usually sat on the other end of the dugout from Gil—like when you were a kid, you didn't want to sit in the front row and have the teacher looking right at you. Likewise, Gil and Rube were always in the front seat of the bus to the ballpark on the road, so we sat in the back.

I remember Gil pitched batting practice that day, as he often did. I saw in the Gil Hodges biography that he threw BP that night in Atlanta even though he wasn't feeling well; he wanted to toss some knuckleballs to get the Mets ready to face Phil Niekro, who would win that night. Not many managers in the majors threw batting practice, but Gil liked to and felt it kept him in shape. This time it didn't help anyone.

Jerry Koosman started that game in Atlanta and was sent to the showers after six innings. When Kooz went into the clubhouse after he was pinch-hit for, he saw Gil lying in the trainer's room. The idea of Gil not being on the bench while a game was going on was jarring, but seeing him lying down, all red in the face and not looking good, was unnerving. Gil was taken to the hospital a little while later, and tests confirmed that he had suffered a heart attack. His wife, Joan, flew down immediately.

It was a long time before anyone from the press or the team saw Gil. He spent that winter in Florida, and no one really had much contact with him until shortly before spring training started. Despite the scare about his health, Gil showed up in St. Petersburg rested and geared up for the 1969 season. All of us were ready.

Chapter 3

THE 100–1 SHOT

A Different Kind of Ball

We had a basketball team in the off-season. I can't say it was a Mets team, because we had baseball players from several teams on it, and Ed Kranepool picked who was on the team. Eddie got ballplayers who were local, who wanted to play, and who wanted to make $100 apiece in a game.

We played anywhere we could make that $100: Long Island, Westchester, and other areas around New York. Players included Jeff Torborg, Bill Robinson, Bill Monbouquette, Al Jackson, Kranepool, Jack Lamabe, and me. Only Jackson, Krane, and I were Mets at the time. The other guys fit in by being in the area and by being available to play. The team was called Art Baumgarten's Major League All-Stars, and we had our names on the front of our jerseys. I don't remember how we all came together, but what I do remember is that Art Baumgarten was Krane's friend—and we usually won.

Monbouquette was a pretty good pitcher for the Red Sox, and he wound up pitching for the Yankees in 1968. Lamabe was from Farmingdale, Long Island, and he played for a number of teams, including the Mets in 1967. Bill Robinson was a young outfielder for the Yankees; he had a long career, mostly with the Pirates and Phillies. Robinson and Monbouquette were later Mets coaches. Torborg was from New Jersey and was a catcher for the Dodgers in the 1960s. He managed several teams later on—including the Mets.

Some of the guys—such as Krane, who grew up in the Bronx—were really good high school basketball players. I played pickup basketball in high school and loved it. Basketball was a great way to stay in shape for baseball in the spring. I didn't think I was good enough to play at University City High in St. Louis, yet here I was traveling all over the Tri-State area playing basketball for money! Krane was a little taller than me—he was the big man.

When we played the Jets' team, they tried to beat up on us. We had something in common: Shea Stadium. Joe Namath didn't play against us. It seemed like it was always linebackers and tackles—and plenty of contact.

We played basketball a lot during the winter following the 1968 season, when my family and I first moved to the city. After 1969 we were so busy we didn't play basketball anymore; we had so many other appearances that we didn't have to sweat to make a buck—or a bucket.

I don't remember the Mets or Gil Hodges saying anything one way or the other about spending the winter playing basketball. The team probably felt it was a good way to stay in shape and let us earn some extra money in the off-season. I recently learned in the Gil Hodges biography *Gil Hodges: The Brooklyn Bums, the Miracle Mets, and the Extraordinary Life of a Baseball Legend,* by Tom Clavin and Danny Peary, that Gil played basketball as a college student in Indiana in the winter when he was breaking in with the Brooklyn Dodgers. He was pretty good and—not surprisingly—a team leader. Gil was inducted into the Oakland City University Hall of Fame in 2024—for basketball!

Division Play

When spring training started in 1969, nobody had any idea what was going to happen. Each league had just added two teams and split into two divisions. This was something entirely new, and we were all a little apprehensive about what was happening. The Las Vegas oddsmakers weren't impressed with us: Vegas listed 100-to-1 odds on the Mets winning the World Series.

Gil told us, "I don't know if you know this, but we lost around 37 one-run games last year—the most in the league. Just think about this: If you win a few of those, what happens? If you win more than a few, what happens? How do we do that? We find ways to win. We've got good pitching and we've got good defense. Find ways to win games."

That is about as simple a philosophy as you could imagine. And by summer, we started to find ways to win those close games. It just took time to get through our thick skulls that he was completely right. That was part of the greatness of Gil. His way of managing was getting everyone involved. Everyone on that team felt like an integral part of the whole.

And yet on a personal level, Gil was tough. I avoided him as much as possible. He wasn't someone who would pat you on the back if you did something well, and he didn't chastise you if you did something bad, especially in front of other players. He wasn't going to waste a lot of words on us. Or umpires.

I don't recall ever seeing him get thrown out of a game, though the record shows it happened a couple times. Whenever he came out to talk to an umpire during the game, he made his point and then walked slowly back to the dugout. Many times when I played first base, I'd look at him and he would give me a sign regarding holding a base runner on. There was not a lot of verbal communication.

Gil had one of two ways to let you know he wanted you to go into the game—neither of which required much conversation. If I were at the end of the bench, he'd just get up and walk about halfway down the dugout. I'd see him coming, and he'd stop and just point at me. That was all he had to do. Other times you might hear "Sham" or "Shamsky" from one of the coaches, which is how he often passed on what he wanted. Simple communication. Not fancy but effective.

Expo-nsion

Jerry Koosman was one poor outing away from winning 20 games in his first full season in 1968—and he was one vote short of matching Reds catcher Johnny Bench as National League Rookie of the Year. Kooz was so good he was in consideration to start the season opener in 1969. He sat down with Rube Walker and talked about it, but Kooz said he told Rube that it didn't really matter and it was maybe better that Tom Seaver do it. Seaver had been Rookie of the Year in 1967, and he was very popular. Koosman was fine with it.

So Seaver started at Shea against the expansion Montreal Expos in their first-ever game to open the 1969 season. It was probably Tom's worst start of what became a remarkable season. He didn't get tagged with the decision (Cal Koonce took the *L*), but an 11–10 defeat to a brand-new team is not how you want to start a season.

Tom's 25 wins in 1969 are still a Mets record. The way the game is played now, 25 wins will probably remain the most in a season by a Met forever—as is the case with many of Seaver's records.

Back-to-Back

I missed almost all of spring training in 1969. I hurt my back working out at first base early in spring training and started the season on the disabled list. When I was better and it was time for me to come off the disabled list, I made a stupid remark in a meeting with GM Johnny Murphy and Gil Hodges, telling them, "I don't need spring training to play on this team." I knew right away I had messed up. Their idea of sending me to the minors to get ready made sense—it's standard procedure now for a player coming off an injury. But my response at the time came out of frustration and disappointment that I couldn't just go out there and play in New York. As soon as I said it, I knew it was uncalled for, especially to these two men who had been very fair to me. And I hadn't played at all from the first week of spring training games until about May 1. So that was more than six weeks between getting into any game.

I was so banged up I couldn't even make it to Opening Day at Shea to stand on the line and be announced to the crowd. I really didn't know if I was going to play again—and I'm not just talking about the spring of 1969. I was so depressed and worried. I felt overmatched. I'd hurt my back in 1967, but that was nothing compared to the way it felt in '69. It took me forever to get better. We didn't have the best treatments then, and you just never knew what could happen, but I knew so many people in the game who went from a promising career to never being heard from again. I was desperate. I went to osteopaths, I went to neurosurgeons, I went to chiropractors, I went to acupuncturists—all on my own.

During the time I dealt with my back issues, I tried everything. There was one doctor on Park Avenue who would charge $25 per visit and treated every patient the same way: sit in a chair and he would insert cotton swabs up each nostril. I'm pretty sure it was medical cocaine. It was interesting, but it didn't help much. I also then flew to Boston and saw the doctor who supposedly treated John F. Kennedy for his back issues. A friend made the arrangements and flew up on the shuttle with me, which was good, because after the intravenous injection the doctor gave me, I was completely out of it coming home. In most of these cases, I felt better when I left, but it didn't last.

Art Heyman, the number-one draft choice in the NBA by the Knicks in 1963, was a New York kid who was an All-American at Duke and is still revered down there. By the late 1960s he had had moved to the ABA. Whenever I ran into him, we would commiserate about our back problems. He tried even more remedies than I did. One day he told me, "I've got a friend who's now involved in acupuncture." It was just starting to become popular at the time, and Art talked me into going to see this acupuncturist on the Upper East Side. I didn't want needles stuck in me and was apprehensive but also desperate. I convinced myself to go see the acupuncturist, and I was shown to this little room to wait for him. I looked at the framed certificate on the wall. It said that he was certified: "[Having] completed six weeks of training, the graduate is deemed certified in acupuncture." I gathered up my things, got right out of there, and never looked back. I was desperate enough to try anything, but six weeks was a little too soon to have someone sticking needles in my body.

The truth was, I just had to wait it out. In the same amount of time it took for Art Heyman's buddy to get his acupuncture certificate, my back began to feel better. When I was able to play, the idea of getting ready by going to the minors felt like a setback. It wasn't. That's what Whitey Herzog told me in April 1969.

The future Hall of Fame manager was the Mets farm director in '69—his knowledge and understanding of the organization was an underappreciated part of the success we had that year. Whitey called me after my regrettable meeting with Gil and Murphy and smoothed everything over. He told me, "It's nothing bad. Just go down to Tidewater and get some at-bats. Don't pay attention to any of this stuff. Just get your work in, and you'll be right back."

It was perfect advice for me. I guess I could have stayed with the Mets, but who knows if I would have been able to get the work in that I needed? And Whitey was right: I did come right back.

It also helped that Dave Rosenfield was general manager at Tidewater. He had been GM when I played at Topeka in the Class B Three-I League in the Reds system. The Mets had just taken over the team—located in Norfolk, Virginia—and Dave would oversee the Triple-A Tides for their 37 years as a Mets affiliate, winning International League Executive of the Year four times. With Dave looking out for me in Tidewater, I felt a lot more comfortable. He pretty much told me the same things Whitey had told me. It was good to have those assurances, because it's a shock going to the minors after establishing yourself in the big leagues. Nobody wants to get hurt in Florida and miss spring training—and nobody wants to go back down to the minors to get into playing shape. You do it because it's the best way to get ready.

I played 11 games in Tidewater, had nine extra-base hits, and batted .290. Ten days later I was back in New York. My first at-bat in 1969 was against Atlanta on May 13. I singled up the middle to drive in the run in the ninth inning against Cecil Upshaw. Gil had gone through his bench that night and sent Tom Seaver in to run for me in a one-run game. I think he was trying to protect me from getting hurt again—pulling a muscle or something. Tom wasn't too fast, but he was more valuable than anyone on the team. So it was probably another bit of 1969 Mets luck that the next batter made the last out of the game and Tom didn't have to risk an injury trying to score.

We lost, but it was a big thrill getting a hit in my first at-bat in a tight game. My season had finally started. There was another added benefit. Since I did not start the year on the roster, Rod Gaspar made the team instead and established himself as a key player who filled in all over the place. He actually played more games than I did in 1969, but I had about 100 more at-bats and was the only Mets regular besides Cleon Jones to hit .300 that year. Rod has never stopped thanking me for my bad back getting him on the team. His career may not have been that long, but it certainly was eventful.

Road Warrior: Lou Niss

The creation of the Montreal Expos in 1969 added international travel to our itinerary. Traveling secretary Lou Niss was not phased at all. Lou actually predated the Mets. In 1959 Branch Rickey was named president of the Continental League, which Bill Shea put together when the National League wasn't initially thrilled with the idea of expansion. Rickey hired Lou, who'd been sports editor at the *Brooklyn Eagle*, to handle public relations. It worked because the Mets were added as an expansion team, and the Continental League folded before it began.

Lou was hired as traveling secretary when the Mets joined the National League—the team even put out a press release before he retired in 1980 claiming him as the team's first employee. It was a demanding job, but Lou was an expert at not letting the travel details and paperwork make him crazy. Lou had a hearing aid in one ear, and as I got to know him, I realized he had developed selective hearing in *both* ears about any complaints that pertained to travel; these included air travel, hotel accommodations, long-distance bus travel, buses to and from the ballpark, equipment left behind, and luggage not arriving on time.

There were always a few players who would complain about buses not leaving on time. That's where the selective hearing would come in—that was one of his best qualities. It wasn't a simple task to be traveling secretary and keep a party of 35 or more people happy—or at least quiet—while we spent six months crisscrossing the country.

Road Fashion by Donn Clendenon

There are two parts to this. One: wearing a jacket and tie was Gil Hodges's rule. And two: we had to listen to Donn Clendenon tell us how ugly our clothes were. He went on and on about how bad we looked in our sports coats or suits— whatever we wore, he was ready to tear us down.

Donn arrived in New York from Montreal at the trade deadline, which was June 15 in 1969, and for many years before and after that. Our general manager, Johnny Murphy, got Clendenon as a big bat and also for his veteran leadership for our very young team. A big part of that leadership was keeping everyone loose. He did that the way a lot of ballplayers did: by getting on everybody as often as possible.

If you're trying to come up with comebacks as someone relentlessly hounds you about how ugly your clothes are, you aren't dwelling so much on having to face Fergie Jenkins or Bob Gibson, or on that tough road trip coming up. And there's a good chance that our clothes weren't so fashionable. None of us were fashionistas like Clyde Frazier on the Knicks. We weren't making enough money to buy really nice clothes.

When Clendenon would get on you, it's not like he would come up next to you and say, "Man, that's the ugliest suit I've ever seen." You'd be at your locker in a sports coat and tie, and he would yell it across the room for everybody in the clubhouse to hear.

His contempt wasn't just reserved for your clothes on the road. It was your uniform too! Your pants might have been a little too baggy for Donn's liking. And you had to get back on him for stuff; otherwise he would never stop.

I never talked with Donn when he was with Pittsburgh or in his short time with Montreal. When he was with us—it was probably his first day there—he saw me and realized who I was. Then he immediately started chirping about the series in which I hit four home runs over two games for the Reds at Crosley Field in 1966, which was against the Pirates. I came into the game in the eighth inning, hit a home run, and then homered my next two times up as the game went 13 innings. I homered my next time up in my next game, which wasn't for two days. I'm sure Donn didn't forget to note that his Pirates beat the Reds in both games despite all my home runs.

Donn did say—ad nauseam—how he was still disappointed his team didn't hit me, didn't throw at me, and all this other stuff I had to listen to. He never stopped—all about if he were managing, he would have done this and he would have done that. That was something he always got on me about. This might sound strange, but I miss all that. I miss Donn.

Getting Hot

In the summer of 1969, we were still many games behind the Cubs, but we had a belief that if we could stay close, we could compete. We weren't thinking of winning the division, the pennant, or the World Series at that point. If we had good pitching, good fielding, and some timely hitting, we could start winning close games and stay in the race. It took three and a half more months to get everything together. We were getting confident. We had some good rookies and guys who hadn't been around that long who played like veterans. It was the second year on the Mets for me, as well as for Tommie Agee, Al Weis, and J. C. Martin. Not to mention Gil Hodges's second year at the helm.

It took us about three months to get going and see what we could do. Then once we acquired Donn Clendenon at the June 15 trading deadline, we really started clicking. We were platooning, more or less, at five positions: first base, second base, third base, right field, and sometimes catcher—for the most part. Gil made sure Jerry Grote got regular rest behind the plate and used veteran J. C. Martin a lot, as well as rookie Duffy Dyer, to keep Jerry fresh.

Though there were a lot of memorable games during the 1969 season—people always bring up Tom Seaver's "imperfect game," during which the Cubs broke up his bid for a perfect game in the ninth—I don't think it was one game that changed our season. We had a strong manager in Gil, who told us we needed to start winning some close games. And he was right—it was the big difference. We knew how to lose close games; we needed to learn how to win them. And that was the key.

Moon over Montreal

We split a four-game series at Jarry Park in Montreal on July 20, 1969. We all just wanted to get back home. It was the All-Star break, and most of us had the next three days off, but we were stuck at the airport. Our plane had mechanical issues, and we had no idea how long we'd have to wait. All of us were frustrated, like most people would be in that situation. There was something good on TV, though: the moon landing.

It was quite a time. I don't know if any of us thought the significance would carry on for so many years. The bulk of the players and coaches were crowded into the airport bar watching every moment. Maybe a couple of guys snuck off and did something else—we were there for a while. You found out who was really into the space race and who was just killing time. I'll say most of the guys were into it, fixated by the drama of men walking on the moon. It wasn't like any of us could go home, or ask the bartender to turn the channel! We were a captive audience.

Had our plane to New York taken off as scheduled, we probably would have been in the air and missed the big event when it actually happened. The race for space superiority and being the first country to pull off the moon landing was a major deal. With all the effort put into making this happen, stepping foot on the moon was an incredible accomplishment. The significance of the moment had most of us mesmerized. And not just at the Montreal airport.

The moon landing was such a positive milestone for America at the time. The country was in a funk. I think one of the reasons why the 1969 Mets still resonate with so many people is that numerous unpleasant things were going on at the time—especially in the cities, with war protests, strikes, and violence in the streets over multiple years—and a lot of people were glad there was some good news. Fans still come up to me today and just say "Thank you."

While working on my first book, *The Magnificent Seasons* (published in 2004), I spent hours at the New York Public Library looking through microfiche. I looked at many different newspapers from 1968 to 1969, going through what was happening in the news to accompany everything at Shea that year. The Jets had won the AFL championship at Shea and the Super Bowl in Miami three months before we took the field in 1969. There was a lot of great sports news in New York— the Knicks won their first NBA title in the 1969–70 season, for example—but I was rarely able to find anything you'd call happy news in any other sections of the papers. It was always bad news: deaths in Vietnam, problems in the cities, Nixon's first year in office—the list went on and on.

Yet landing on the moon was thrilling, because it made people proud of this massive accomplishment by the government and NASA. It seems easy to talk about it now, that the landing on the moon was inevitable, but it took so many people at NASA to handle the technological developments and make sure everything went perfectly. Americans felt that we as a country had done something special. And as the years have gone on, it's proven to be something uniquely special. As of this writing, no one has walked on the moon since 1972, though we have made unmanned landings there recently.

There are indeed a few accomplishments from 1969 that are still worth savoring.

The Long Walk

In 1969 Cleon Jones was as good a hitter as anyone in base-ball. Cleon batted .340—a franchise record for about three decades—and wound up third in the National League in hit-ting that year behind Pete Rose and Roberto Clemente. But what happened on July 30 that year wasn't about his bat, and it changed the team for the better.

I was standing in right field as we were getting our butts kicked by Houston—again. The Astros weren't a great team, but they beat us badly that year. We went 2–10 against them in 1969. Houston was the one team we couldn't beat. We'd been rained out the night before, and we had a makeup doubleheader for a previous rainout scheduled. The field was still very wet.

The Astros had an 11-run ninth inning in the first game to blow open a close ballgame—the final score was 16–3. It was the most runs we allowed in a game all year (the third-most comprised the 11 the Astros scored in the nightcap of that dou-bleheader!). In the third inning of that second game, Houston scored 10 runs. I've still never seen two innings like that in one day in the major leagues. Johnny Edwards, a left-handed-hitting catcher who was a teammate of mine in Cincinnati, hit a fly ball into the left-field corner. Cleon chased after it. It wasn't a pretty play, and it wasn't a pretty day for the Mets.

After the play, I thought Gil Hodges was going to the mound to talk to Nolan Ryan, who had just come on in relief. When Hodges would come out to the mound, he never stepped on the baseline. Like a lot of ballplayers—myself included—he was a little superstitious that way.

Back then my eyes were really good. I could watch the ball come out of the pitcher's hand and almost see the writing on it. And this time when Gil came out to walk on the field, he must have missed stepping on the baseline by half an inch, like he wasn't even paying attention. And Gil always paid attention. When he walked past the pitcher, heading toward shortstop, I wondered, "What did Buddy do?"

And then he walked by Buddy. I said, "Oh, my God. If I were Cleon I would just run toward that door in the left-field fence, go into the bullpen, and just get out of there." That was my first reaction. Of course, Cleon stood there and waited for Gil to make the long walk out there. I obviously couldn't hear what they were talking about, but I believe Gil tugged on Cleon's uniform very gently. That's the way I saw it. A moment later Cleon left his position, following a few steps behind Gil. Ron Swoboda came out and took Cleon's spot in left field.

To this day, Cleon says Gil was just asking how he was feeling. Cleon told him, "You know that I hurt my ankle up in Montreal. Look at how wet it is out here." Gil agreed with him, and Cleon recalled him saying, "You know what, you've got a bad ankle anyway, and you shouldn't even be out here. I think you ought to come out of the ballgame." Cleon said he didn't think that much about it after he went into the dugout, and the newspapers made it into a story. We were outscored 27–8 that day, so there weren't a lot of positive things for the press to write about.

Ron Swoboda's Time

From a team standpoint, though, what came out of that moment with Cleon Jones and Gil Hodges was a twofold thing. It got us to understand that there was no nonsense, which we knew anyway. Gil was not happy. If he could take out a player hitting about .350 at the time, that told us all we'd better stay alert and be on top of our game at all times. The other thing Gil's walk out to left field did was give Ron Swoboda an opportunity to play.

Swoboda hadn't been playing much. Now that Cleon needed a few days off, Ronnie got in a groove and came on strong. I know his batting average was not great the rest of the season—.234—but he wound up with more playing time, got his confidence up, and had some huge hits for us.

"Quite honestly I could have been on a cruise, and they wouldn't have missed me," Ron said about the weeks leading up to that game against Houston. "When Hodges started walking out toward the pitcher after Johnny Edwards hit the ball to left field and the play was over, I—like everyone—thought Gil was going to the mound. Then he walked past the pitcher. I thought, *What is he going to say to Bud Harrelson at shortstop?* But when he walked past Buddy toward Cleon, I just thought, thankfully, it was better Cleon than me. As he walked back with Cleon, Gil said, 'Swoboda, you're in.' It took me a few seconds because I couldn't find my hat or glove. Turns out I ended up with two hits in that game, started to play more, and hit a lot better. I got on a roll and ended up having a good World Series."

Swoboda's biggest game down the stretch was the night in St. Louis when Steve Carlton struck out a record 19 batters, yet we still beat the future Hall of Famer. Even though Ron struck out twice, he took Carlton deep with a man on in his other two at-bats to win a huge September ballgame 4–3.

What really got me, though, was that Ron got batting tips from Ralph Kiner before that game. I finally asked Ronnie about it. "After Ralph's help and my success in that game, I felt like I could hit anybody," Ron said. "Ralph talked to me about a few things, and I wish I would have been able to talk to him much more about hitting over the years. There wasn't a hitting coach on our team then, so I will always be thankful for Ralph Kiner's help."

For whatever reason, the Mets were dead set against players getting batting tips, especially from Ralph. We had no batting coach, and a bunch of young players really could have used the help. I wish Ralph would have talked to me about hitting. I was very shy and was reluctant to approach an all-time great such as Ralph. He was an icon to me, a kid growing up and watching him all those years with Pittsburgh.

Ron wasn't worried. He asked Ralph for help, and he had the game of his life. Swoboda had a great finish in 1969. After that terrible series we had at Shea against the Astros in July, we went 34–14 in the games Ron played the rest of the regular season.

The tiebreaking run in the deciding World Series game at Shea? Swoboda drove that in with a double in the eighth inning. Then he came around and scored the insurance run. And of course, there was his unbelievable catch that saved the day in Game 4.

The Shea Advantage

Were teams intimidated coming to Shea Stadium? With Tom Seaver or Jerry Koosman pitching, opponents were facing guys who were in the top tier of the National League. Yet at the same time, there were top-notch pitchers all over the league. So I don't know if *intimidated* is the right word. We certainly didn't have an overpowering hitting team, so opponents weren't intimidated by that.

When we started to play the kind of ball we began playing midway through August 1969, we were as good as anybody in either league. If they came to New York facing Seaver, Koosman, and Gentry, that was pretty tough. Nolan Ryan as the starter in the second game of a doubleheader? That's not something any opponent looked forward to. Teams knew they would be in for a battle when they came to Shea—even in 1968, when our record wasn't good but we still had one of the lowest ERAs in the National League. I think as we started playing better, other teams started to respect us more and look at us differently.

In 1969 we were in most games because of our pitching and defense. I think a lot of people underestimated our defense. We were terrific up the middle with Jerry Grote catching, Ken Boswell and Al Weis platooning at second base, Bud Harrelson at shortstop, and Tommie Agee in center field. We were second in the league to the Braves in fewest errors, with 122.

As we started to become contenders, the crowds at Shea really got involved in the games. The fans were so hungry for good stuff that they really embraced our team. Not like we were close the year before—or any of the years before that. There was not much to cheer about, and they were used to the Mets being out of it. That changed in 1969.

Once they felt like things were turning around, there was an incredible feeling at the ballpark. When I'd go out to right field to start the game, I could see the subway stop for Shea and witness hordes of people running to get into the ballpark because they didn't want to miss the first pitch. When Jane Jarvis played the national anthem on the organ, the crowd would get so revved up halfway through it you could hear the intensity building. It was such an exciting time. Fans had nothing to cheer about in those early years, and suddenly the Mets were not only contenders but the hottest team in baseball. Suddenly every series was important.

The stands were packed most nights, and fans were rewarded for their dedication. We were 9–1 against the West Coast teams in our last August home stand, 8–1 on our next trip home, and after starting the last home stand of the regular season at 0–3, we didn't lose again until the last day of the season.

We drew almost 2.2 million to Shea in 1969, the most in the major leagues. Because of a lot of rainouts, we had only 70 home dates and a lot of doubleheaders—single-admission doubleheaders were the only kind there were. Average attendance after August 15 was more than 35,000 per game, with 11 out of 20 dates drawing 40,000 or more.

We were on a roll, and I think what happened to us became contagious. Everybody on the team started to feel important, because everybody contributed at some point.

Chicago Showdown

On August 13, 1969, we were 10 games behind the Cubs. When the Cubs arrived at Shea on September 8, we were just 2 ½ games back. Those were incredible games for the fans. We had a heated rivalry that really started with Leo Durocher. Leo was laughing at us and taking every occasion to put down what we were doing. The night after Tom Seaver's "imperfect game" in July 1969, a reporter asked him, when Chicago salvaged a win, "Are those the real Cubs?" Leo shot back, "Those are the real Mets!"

That rivalry certainly benefited from the stark difference between the way Leo went about his business with the Cubs and how Gil did things with the Mets. Interestingly, Leo was Gil's first manager when he came up with the Brooklyn Dodgers. He was the one who first gave Gil a first baseman's mitt—Gil had come up through the minor leagues as a catcher. Leo ran hot and cold; Gil was stoic, reserved, always thinking.

You could see Leo's influence over the Cubs players, with Ron Santo clicking his heels after Cubs wins in '69. I asked Ron about that for *Magnificent Seasons*, and he said Leo wanted him to do it. Santo said he only did it on Sundays at home when they won. It sure seems like he did it a lot more than that.

Santo was their leader. When Cubs starter Bill Hands came in on Tommie Agee in the first inning of the showdown at Shea, Jerry Koosman drilled Santo in the arm to start the second inning. Agee hit a two-run homer his next time up and scored the deciding run on a close play at the plate.

The Black Cat

The next night—August 14, 1969—the black cat emerged from nowhere and sauntered in front of the Cubs dugout. I remember I was so happy that the cat didn't come over and stare at us on our side, because that would have freaked me out. The whole thing was bizarre! Johnny McCarthy was head of the grounds crew then. Pete Flynn, who was hired by McCarthy when the Mets started at the Polo Grounds in 1962, stayed with the Mets for their first 50 seasons. I talked to Pete many times, and he said the grounds crew never saw the cat before that day, and they never saw it again after the Cubs left town.

Fergie Jenkins was pitching for the Cubs that night. We've been friends for years, and he did tell me once that he was glad the cat didn't come over and stare at him either. The cat just stared at manager Leo Durocher in the dugout. It slowly walked away and then disappeared. Likewise, the Cubs soon disappeared from the top of the National League East.

Having lived in New York for a long time, I've seen everything when it comes to animals living on their own: cat colonies, rat colonies, raccoon colonies, snakes. Who knows what was underneath a stadium that was built on a trash heap?

Superstition

I do know that most athletes—especially baseball players—are very superstitious. So I can't imagine anybody not being affected if that black cat were looking right at them. Especially given the importance of those games with the Cubs. After winning that first game of the series at Shea on that Monday, we were only one and a half games out with less than a month left in the season. Those were key games. And we ended up pounding the Cubs in that last game of the two-game series when the black cat appeared. We swept a doubleheader from Montreal the next night and went into first place.

Why are ballplayers so superstitious? Sports in general—and baseball in particular—are all about streaks. If I had a good game, I would take my bats home with me. Especially if it meant that it kept pitchers from using them during batting practice. Though that may fall more in the category of wisdom than superstition.

I would drive to the ballpark home and back the same way if had a good game. Again, if I were in a slump, I'd drive home any old way.

I tried to eat the same foods if I had a good game. I know about Wade Boggs eating chicken because one day after he ate chicken, he had a good game. Boggs wound up with 3,000 hits, so he ate chicken all the time. I didn't have as many hits—and maybe I wasn't as superstitious as Boggs—but if I had chicken the day of the game and then got two or three hits, you can bet I'd be eating the same thing the next day. Tongue. Liver. Chipped beef. If it resulted in a good night at the plate, I'd put anything on my plate again the next night.

Even though we were pretty set with what Hodges was doing in 1969 in terms of who would start if a lefty or a righty were pitching the next day, I'd still eat the same thing the day after a big game. With Gil, you never knew when you were going to get in. And against the Pirates that day in 1966 when I was with the Reds, I didn't start one day and still ended up hitting three home runs when the game went into extra innings. You never knew when your time might come—and you never knew which superstition would come into play. I would keep up the superstitions no matter what.

Listening on the Radio in Pittsburgh

You do things in life that you can't explain. I had never before or after asked a manager to sit out the first of the High Holy Days on the Jewish calendar. I was not overly religious, but for whatever reason, I felt I had to do that at the time. Gil was very fair and said he supported my decision. But I have to say that I was on pins and needles during both games in Pittsburgh. The Mets had been in first place for all of two days, and this was when I decided to sit out.

I was really praying we didn't lose that doubleheader. I could have dealt with a split, but if we lost two games, I really thought I was going to get hate mail and all sorts of negative stuff. I would have felt like I had done something wrong.

The team sent pitchers Don Cardwell and Jerry Koosman ahead to Pittsburgh while we were at Shea playing Montreal. Gary Gentry pitched a complete-game shutout against the Expos. We traveled to Pittsburgh that night. Two right-handers were scheduled in the Friday doubleheader for the Pirates— Bob Moose and Dock Ellis—and based on our platoon system, I would have started both games. Donn Clendenon batted cleanup instead of me, and Ron Swoboda played right field in my spot—Donn reached base three times that night and Ron had a hit in each game of the doubleheader. But the big story was a unique bit of fortune overcoming our lack of hitting in both games to win by identical 1–0 scores.

It was nerve-racking for me sitting in my hotel room and listening to those two tight games against a hard-hitting Pirates team. A part of Mets lore is that on this night our starting pitchers drove in the only run in each of the two games. How good was our pitching in that stretch? That sweep gave us three shutouts in a row and four in the week when we took over first place.

Cardwell's run-scoring hit in the second game was not a shock; Don had good power and had 15 home runs in his career. He threw four-hit ball for eight innings, with Tug McGraw getting Mets-killer Willie Stargell to fly out and future batting champ Al Oliver to ground out with the tying run on base in the ninth.

Jerry, by his own confession, was not a good hitter. So for Kooz to pitch so effectively and drive in the only run of the game for his *only RBI of the year* in a crucial series on a night when both pitchers drove in the only runs—while I was sweating it out in a hotel room—makes it an even more unbelievable story. I mean, Koosman hit .048 that year!

Though I wasn't in the clubhouse that day, I heard Cardwell and Koosman carping at each other forever about which of them hit the ball harder in driving in the only runs of those two games in Pittsburgh. That night goes along with all the unexplainable things that happened to us in 1969.

I reported for duty the next day and found a sign in my locker saying, "We won two games without you. Why don't you stay out the rest of the year?" I never found out for sure, but that certainly sounded like the work of Clendenon to me.

Unfortunately for me, the Pirates threw a lefty on Saturday and because of the platoon system I was relegated to the bench. Tom Seaver pitched us to our 10th straight victory. The following weekend at Shea, the same two Mets pitchers–turned–RBI machines—Jerry and Don—pitched again against the same team, and I was able to contribute in both games. I felt a lot better about being in the lineup and helping them win.

The Last Out in Shea's Last No-Hitter

Shea Stadium was around for 45 seasons. You may recall that no Met ever pitched a no-hitter at Shea—or anyplace else—until the team moved to Citi Field. Shea did see a couple no-hitters, however. Just 31 games into the stadium's existence, Philadelphia's Jim Bunning famously tossed a perfect game on Father's Day at Shea in 1964. (It was the first perfect game in the National League since 1880.)

The hapless 1962 Mets had also been no-hit at Dodger Stadium by Sandy Koufax in 1962; those early Mets teams were so bad, it's surprising they weren't no-hit more often. In 1969, though, everything we did seemed to turn out right. Just a few days before we saw him, Steve Carlton had struck out a record 19 batters against us in St. Louis, yet we won on Ron Swoboda's two two-run homers in between his two strikeouts against Carlton. By September 20 we already had won 91 games and had a four-game lead.

That weekend we were in a little bit of a funk. After winning 13 out of 14 to dash past the Cubs into first place, the Pirates hammered us in back-to-back games at Shea on April 16 and 17, sweeping the Friday night games by a combined score of

16–2. Saturday's pitcher, Bob Moose—just 21 years old and used more often as a reliever than a starter—didn't allow us to get any hits at all. Roberto Clemente made a running catch in right field on a liner by Wayne Garrett to save the no-hitter. As fate would have it, I was the last batter Moose faced. I grounded out to second to end the game.

That no-hitter was typical of that year and the strange things that happened. You couldn't explain it. Moose's no-hitter was the last loss we had at Shea in 1969. Even stranger is that it was the last no-hitter ever thrown at Shea, a great park for pitchers that was around for 39 more seasons.

Left, Right, Left

Gil Hodges challenged me as a player, whether it was hitting grounders at first base like he was trying to hurt me or letting me take an at-bat against a lefty reliever late in a key game. He was a terrific manager. Gil loved to platoon, but it wasn't automatic. In 1969 I batted 24 times against lefties. I hit .409 against lefties that year; I never thought I was at a disadvantage against them.

After being no-hit by Bob Moose, we wrapped up the crucial five-game September series with the Pirates with a Sunday doubleheader at Shea. We had dropped three straight to Pittsburgh and were fortunate that the Cubs had dropped 14 of 18—including two to us—and our lead held at four games.

For the Sunday doubleheader at Shea, we had the same two pitchers who had won the two 1–0 games in Pittsburgh the previous week: Jerry Koosman and Don Cardwell. Dock Ellis, who'd lost the second game of that doubleheader in Pittsburgh on the single by Cardwell, wasn't as sharp as he'd been at Forbes Field. In the bottom of the seventh, the Pirates brought in veteran lefty Joe Gibbon. We were up by a run. Gil had all us lefties bat against the southpaw: Garrett, Boswell, Kranepool, and me. I homered for a key insurance run. We won the first game 5–3.

I started the second game too. I went 2-for-3 against Steve Blass, a tough right-hander. Once again I had an at-bat against a lefty reliever, Lou Marone. I hit the ball pretty well off him, a fly to center field that was deep enough to be a sacrifice fly and put us up 6–1. Cardwell went the distance and we swept the doubleheader. That day started a nine-game winning streak that wrapped up the division title for us. Take away those three straight losses to the Pirates at Shea, and we won 19 games in a row.

Each win was a little different, but they all followed a single principle: Gil did it his way. He wasn't your basic manager and would not follow the book or whatever you want to call it. He'd do things based on his idea about the game, and he was successful.

Using so many position players and having a hard-throwing pitching staff made the difference in the doubleheaders that piled up due to early season rainouts. We went 11–3–8 in doubleheaders in 1969. Put all the games in all those doubleheaders together, and that's a 30–14 record (.681 win percentage). We had six sweeps in our last nine doubleheaders, starting our turnaround from 10 games back on August 16. Doubleheaders were all single-admission back then, so despite only having 70 home dates, we still drew the most fans in baseball: 2,175,373.

More Platooning

I think what happens is that earlier in your career, you get labeled, whether you like it or not. Gil was having so much success in righty-lefty platooning that he just stayed with it. In the long run, it hurt our careers, unfortunately. I look at it as positively as I can: it gave me the opportunity to play on a championship team.

When I meet people today, nobody mentions the platoon or says, "You didn't play this day; you didn't play that day." They just think of me as playing on that team. When I think about my career, it has always bothered me that I wasn't able to put up the numbers I think I should have.

Whenever I went 0-for-4 or 0-for-3, I wasn't sure if I'd play the next day. That kind of pressure for a big-league ballplayer is almost unbearable, but it is what it is—or was what it was.

Ken Boswell was my roommate, and he shared the same feeling. He was platooning with Al Weis. It turned out Al was a hero in the World Series, but Al was a really good defensive player and not a terrific hitter, which even he would tell you. Gil had a lot of confidence in him, and it certainly worked out.

I think the other two left-handed parts of the platoon, Ed Kranepool and Wayne Garrett, felt the same. These guys were terrific players. It was a positive in a lot of ways, of course. Veteran Ed Charles, a steady influence at third, helped Wayne out as such a young guy. Krane actually had more playing time than Donn Clendenon, the big bat that we acquired in '69, but like everything else, it worked beautifully that year.

"When we acquired Donn Clendenon in June, that set up the whole platoon situation," Cleon Jones told me recently. "Everything fell into place after that. Gil knew what he was doing and got the most out of everyone. He had a vision."

With Ronnie Swoboda and me in right field, Gil received maximum results out of the two of us. I don't remember the day that the platooning really started, but it was pretty early in the year. You put Ron and me together, and you've got quite a hitter. (Remember that I missed the first month of the season with a back injury.)

'69 RF	G	AB	R	H	HR	RBI	BB	AVG	OBP	SLG
Shamsky	100	303	42	91	14	47	36	.300	.375	.488
Swoboda	109	327	38	77	9	52	43	.235	.326	.361
Total		630	80	168	23	99	79	.267	.350	.422

In 1968 we hadn't platooned nearly as much. That year I started 64 games in left field and only 11 in right (plus 13 starts at first base). So if there was anybody I was platooning with, I suppose it would be Cleon Jones—at least for the first half of the year. As 1968 wound down, Cleon played left most of the time, and I was mostly coming off the bench and occasionally started in right field or at first base. Larry Stahl played a lot that year in center and right. Larry wound up going to the San Diego Padres in the expansion draft in October 1968.

Platooning makes it hard to get into a groove. We dealt with it—or at least I dealt with it—because it was still an opportunity to play, and we had the utmost respect for Gil and the way he handled the club.

You've heard plenty from me about platooning; here's what my other half told me: "I felt lucky to be platooning in right field," Ron said. "I was happy to be getting a chance to play." As for me, he noted, "You were having a good year. Earlier in the season, I wasn't doing too well and was not playing much. And when the platooning started, I realized with Gil you never knew what might happen, and to be ready. Platooning is not easy, so you had to be ready."

The Amazing Mets—the Album!

We cut all the songs in one day. And we did it the day after we clinched the National League East title at Shea. We were half hungover! Most of the team was there—even pitching coach Rube Walker was at the studio.

The back of the album says you'll "hear the magic of the champagne-drenched locker room, the incredible electricity of the fans and, as a special surprise, the morning after when the Mets decided to step up to the microphone at Bellsound and take a swing at the recording world."

I can still tell you the titles of all the songs on that album without looking: "The Green Grass of Shea," "God Bless America," "(You've Gotta Have) Heart," and . . . well, I guess I can't tell you the *whole* album from memory. But if you pull *The Amazing Mets* from Buddha Records out of your vintage vinyl collection, you'll see that the track list also includes "Mets—Hallelujah," "Mets Are Here to Stay," "We're Gonna Win the Series," "La La La La," "Locker Room Chatter," "The Mets Ball Game," and "The Song for the '69 Mets," which was sung to the tune of "East Side, West Side" with lyrics from our in-clubhouse poet, Ed Charles. There were a few songs that were adapted from traditional songs like that. Ten songs. That's a lot for a bunch of guys who couldn't sing.

If you still have your copy, it is listed for as much as $200 in some places. So hold on to your copy—or sell it!

Another Trophy in '69: The Mayor's

We went into first for the first time ever on September 10, 1969, against Montreal. And then we clinched exactly two weeks later on September 24 against St. Louis. That was the beginning of three celebrations at Shea, with the field torn up each time. After each celebration, it got a little worse.

The grounds crew did extraordinary work, but you could see patches where they were trying to fill in. In the outfield I could see the remnants of the sections of grass that had been torn up. It was physically impossible to lay down new grass all along the outfield and in the infield. I was amazed how the grounds crew was able to make it playable—it's not like the games weren't important!

What was not so important was an exhibition game. In a strange bit of scheduling, the annual Mayor's Trophy Game was played five days after we clinched the National League East title at Shea in late September. As it happened, the clincher against St. Louis was our last home game on the regular-season schedule. But we still had that exhibition game at Shea against the Yankees in the annual Mayor's Trophy Game.

The Mayor's Trophy Game was usually held in the middle of summer. It was scheduled for early July 1969, but as happened many times that summer, it was rained out. I guess the next available date when both the Mets and Yankees were close to home was 160 games into the season. Exhibition games were always frustrating for the players because they took away a day off. The players always felt they could do without exhibition games during the season. It was even stranger in '69 considering how late it was and how many other things we had on our minds other than a bragging-rights game, even if it was for a good cause.

With us heading to the playoffs, everyone in New York wanting a piece of us, with all kinds of promotions and opportunities, you had to wonder why this game was played at Shea at all. The field had just been torn to pieces by fans who had never seen the Mets play a remotely meaningful game in the team's first seven seasons. The field should have had as many days as possible with no one on it given that the postseason was just days away. I'm not a groundskeeper, but the situation seems bizarre.

Why didn't they just switch the game to Yankee Stadium? I checked the schedule for the 1969 Giants, who still played football at Yankee Stadium then. The Giants had played the Lions in Detroit the previous day, and the Yankees only had two games left on the schedule in the Bronx. It wasn't like Yankee Stadium needed to be converted from football back to baseball or anything.

A story about the Mayor's Trophy Game from the *Daily News* from September 29, 1969, explained that the game featured experimental baseballs that were supposed to have 10 percent more hop than the normal balls. The great baseball writer Red Foley wrote that those "baseball were autographed by Bugs Bunny." The umpires used five dozen rabbit balls before they ran out and switched to regular baseballs.

The rabbit balls did all right by me. I had three hits and knocked in five runs in the 7–6 win over the Yankees. That Mayor's Trophy Game got me in a good groove for the National League Championship Series.

The last two regular-season games against the Cubs that followed the Mayor's Trophy Game were just about as meaningless. Actually the games at Wrigley meant even less, because the Mayor's Trophy Game raised money to support kids in the Police Athletic League in New York. I think PAL was grateful that the teams would do it. It dated back to when the Yankees, Dodgers, and Giants would play each other, starting in 1946, to raise money for youth baseball in New York. The Mayor's Trophy Games petered out in the 1980s, and then teams just wrote checks to support youth baseball.

Looking back, the exhibition game gave us an excuse to come back to New York for a couple days before going from Philadelphia to Chicago on the last road trip. Being home in our own beds certainly beat spending another night in Philadelphia.

As it was, my big night against the Yankees seemed to hone my swing. That game might not have meant anything, but we were so new to the concept of winning—not to mention October baseball—that we needed all the extra work we could get.

100 Wins

By getting hot when we did in 1969, we quickly went from going into first place for the first time ever to clinching our first postseason berth. That made our final trip to Wrigley Field meaningless. Except that if we split that final series with the Cubs, we would finish the year with 100 wins. The Mets were in their third season and second ballpark before they finally won their 100th game as a franchise in 1964. And five years later we had already wrapped up a postseason spot before the final road trip. It was an amazing turnaround!

The papers wouldn't let us forget we were on the verge of another milestone in a season that was full of them. There were between five and seven newspapers regularly covering us—that was still how most people got their news—and the writers let us know that 100 wins was on the horizon. Since we'd clinched, there was no pressure on those games in Chicago, but we wanted to keep winning. We had overtaken the Cubs when they were 10 games up in the middle of August. We put up a .776 winning percentage over our last 49 games (38–11).

We had won eight in a row going into Wrigley. Two of the better lefties in the league were pitching: Jerry Koosman against Kenny Holtzman. Kooz was a rock down the stretch, as, of course, was Seaver—the two combined to win 16 of their last 17 decisions for us in 1969. Kenny Holtzman was a left-handed starter from the same city and same high school as me—University City High School in St. Louis. Since he was four years younger, we weren't on the team at the same time in school. (Coincidentally, Kenny and I ended up on the same team in Oakland at the end of my career.) I only played against Kenny in one game in my major league career, and I had a walk and a rare sacrifice bunt. Against a tough lefty like him, that's not a bad game.

Needless to say, I didn't start the game against him at Wrigley on October 1, 1969. I was still sitting on the bench in the 12th inning when Buddy Harrelson doubled and Tommie Agee moved him to third with a grounder to the right side. Leo Durocher still had his same eight starting players in the game—as he always did—but he'd lifted Holtzman after nine innings. In the 12th inning he had former Mets teammate Dick Selma on the mound. Gil motioned for me to hit for Ron Taylor, and then Durocher came out of the dugout and brought in Hank Aguirre, a lefty. Even as a pinch-hitter in 1969, Gil pulled me back a couple of times and sent up a righty hitter when the team brought in a left-hander. Not this time.

With the postseason coming, maybe Gil was especially interested in seeing what I could do against a lefty. I was always confident when I went up to the plate, whether I was facing a righty or a lefty. Lefties were never a problem for me—I just wanted to hit. I singled to right off Aguirre to bring home Harrelson for what turned out to be our 100th win. I was glad I was able to help make history. We were 27 games better in 1969 than we'd been a year earlier—and 1968, with our 73 wins, had been the best season in Mets history.

It didn't surprise me that I batted in that spot, because Gil was predictably unpredictable. Before we showed up to the ballpark, if we knew who was pitching for the opposition, we had a good idea of who was playing. But not always. I don't think any of the guys who were regulars in the platoon system were surprised by any of Gil's choices. He used his instincts, and we sometimes played when we didn't think we were going to play—I always had to stay ready when I didn't start because Gil loved to use his bench.

The newspaper guys were right: That 100th win was such a milestone to us, even though we'd already won the division. There wasn't pressure in those last games in Chicago, but there was gratification because the Cubs didn't like us and we didn't like them.

The next day, the last day on the regular-season schedule, the Cubs ended our nine-game winning streak—the sixth time we'd won at least six in a row in 1969. But that loss didn't matter a bit. I think I can speak for the whole team by saying how good it felt that last week of the season to be the team on the right side of meaningless games after the way the first seven seasons had ended for the Mets! The next games we'd play in 1969, though, would be plenty meaningful.

Chapter 4

OCTOBER 1969

October Money

The meeting about playoff money was amazing. In 1969 the money collected from the postseason gate was broken into full shares for every player who spent most of the season on the active roster. Players also try to divide some shares to include people who played during the year but were not on the playoff roster.

You learn a lot about people on the day of this meeting. There are guys who want to share money with other people. Someone gets traded or they get hurt or they didn't make the postseason roster, and you sit down and discuss how you want to take care of them. But you always have some who seriously don't want to share much with others—such as the bat boys, the batting practice pitchers, the grounds crew, the traveling secretary, and on and on. All of them come out every day, often getting there long before the players and leaving long after we've gone home. The grounds crew especially saved us in 1969. Without them working around the clock, we wouldn't have even been able to take the field after the fans tore everything up. Yet you always have some players complain about sharing the money they're going to earn.

The players on the active 25-man roster at the time of the meeting come together on their own to discuss who gets what. Managers and coaches aren't at these meetings but get full shares of playoff money. I started the season on the disabled list, but I was still considered on the team from the start of the season.

You make the decision before the postseason starts. You have no idea how far you're going to go. You have a list of the guys who have been there for most of the year, plus the players who were there for part of the year. Sometimes those meetings get heated; sometimes they are smooth.

You might be knocked out in a weekend in the playoffs—the Championship Series was only best-of-five then. Or you might go on to win the World Series like we did.

The 1969 season was the only time I played in the postseason. My last season in the majors was 1972, and my last team was the Oakland A's. I was released in July, and I wasn't part of the first of three straight world championships won by the A's. I did get a cash stipend from Oakland, which was nice because I wasn't there that long. It wasn't exorbitant, but I thought it was a really nice gesture.

Again, you learn a lot about a person during meetings about money!

Marching through Georgia

We went right from Chicago to Atlanta for the playoffs. We had a lot of really young players, so it was good not to have time to think about it. We were young, except for Ron Taylor, Cal Koonce, Don Cardwell, and Donn Clendenon. Their veteran leadership was appreciated. If we all had time to think about what we were about to do or worry about it, who knows if the outcome would have been different. I think it was advantageous to get right into the playoffs. The season ended on Thursday at Wrigley Field, and on Saturday afternoon we were at Atlanta–Fulton County Stadium for the first pitch in National League Championship Series history (a knuckleball by Phil Niekro).

The first game featured two pitchers who would win 300 games each and later go into the Hall of Fame: Niekro and Tom Seaver. I had the first hit in NLCS history to lead off the second inning and scored the first run in this new postseason format, touching home on a single by Jerry Grote. The lead went back and forth, with both starters hanging in despite neither being at the top of his game. Seaver allowed the first home runs in NLCS history—Tony Gonzalez and Hank Aaron each hit one. We scored nine times off Niekro, though only four runs were earned.

Cleon knocked in Wayne Garrett to tie the score in the top of the eighth. I collected my third single of the game. The go-ahead run scored on an error and J. C. Martin, batting for Seaver, hit a crucial two-run single; a third run crossed home on the play on an error. Ron Taylor, our only player with post-season experience, pitched the last two innings of the 9–5 win.

The next day the starting pitching again wasn't ideal, but there was plenty of offense. I was on deck in the seventh inning when Tommie Agee tried to steal home with Cleon at bat. There was no sign. Tommie just took off. Cleon swung and lined the ball foul. It missed Tommie, but not by much. Cleon yelled to Agee, "Just stay there. I'll get you in!" He then homered.

Atlanta's lineup was powerful: Orlando Cepeda, Felipe Alou, Rico Carty, and Hank Aaron, of course. Aaron hit a home run in every game. But we hit the ball as well in that series as we had all year. A team that hit .242 during the year batted .327 and averaged nine runs per game in a sweep.

One thing that is a little frustrating about that series is that barely any footage survives from those first two games in Atlanta. I have seen some film from the third game at Shea—and the celebration that followed. I always wondered why there hasn't been more written about that series with Atlanta. Why is that? It was the first National League Championship Series in baseball history. Very strange. The narrative usually goes something like: "The Mets won 100 during the regular season, swept the Braves in the playoffs, and then went to the World Series." A lot of people saw us as underdogs against Atlanta too. We came from behind to win Games 1 and 3.

Nolan Ryan, Part I

Gil had enough confidence in Nolan Ryan to bring him into key moments in Game 3 in both the playoffs and the World Series. It was not what you would call "by the book."

The Braves were up 2–0 in the third inning with runners on second and third, none out. Rico Carty ripped a ball that was just foul, and while the crowd was still murmuring, Gil walked out of the dugout and—mid-count—called in Nolan. Ryan struck out Carty, a guy who had hit .342 that year and was protecting Hank Aaron in the lineup. Gil had Ryan walk Orlando Cepeda to load the bases and then caught Clete Boyer looking. Bob Didier flew out, and we were out of the jam. We rallied and won the pennant.

Nolan pitched seven innings that day—in relief! Look at the stats from that three-game NLCS: Seaver was the only other Met to throw seven innings in that series. Ryan struck out five more batters than Tom, while Seaver walked one more batter than Ryan. I felt Tom looked out for Nolan like a kid brother. I would say the two of them did pretty well for themselves.

Nolan was a great teammate. He was very young when I first met him in 1968. He could be pretty wild. Gil liked to use him in the second games of doubleheaders or late in games. What probably held him back in his development in New York was that he constantly had to go back to Texas to serve in his army reserve unit during the season, and he had a lot of trouble with blisters on his throwing hand early in his career. He threw so hard, but he couldn't throw strikes consistently. His career took off after the Mets traded him to the Angels and, of course, he became the all-time strikeout leader by a mile—839 Ks to be exact. Nolan is also the all-time leader in walks with 2,795, a staggering 962 more than the next-closest pitcher, Steve Carlton.

One day Nolan was pitching, I was playing first base and Kenny Boswell was playing second. I had a car, and I usually took Ken back to the city, where he would go out and enjoy the New York nightlife of a bachelor ballplayer. And the game just wouldn't end. Nolan was struggling to throw strikes, and when he did throw them, he was throwing so hard the batters kept fouling them off. He was 3–2 on everybody. We were all hoping he would just throw strikes. Ken had his own motives: that night-life I mentioned. After another walk from Ryan, Kenny took a few steps toward the mound and shouted, "Come on, Nolan! Please throw some strikes! I've got a hot date in Manhattan. She's beautiful! Strikes!" I put my glove over my face and just smiled. When I dropped Kenny off in the city after games, I would always remind him if we had a game the next day.

Platoon Overwhelms Braves

The player who wound up the MVP of the 1969 World Series—Donn Clendenon—didn't play at all in the playoffs. Al Weis got a separate national award—the Babe Ruth Award—after the World Series, yet he was the only right-handed platooning batter to get a single at-bat in the NLCS. Charles, Swoboda, and Clendenon all had the playoffs off—and we still swept Atlanta. As Ron Swoboda put it when we talked about the first NLCS: "I was like a bystander. I think I got one scare on the on-deck circle but didn't get an at-bat. It was the most exciting baseball at the time, and quite honestly I was rusty when the World Series started. The fact that I was able to do well in the World Series was a little surprising to me."

How did it work so well with so many good players watching from the dugout? By October, not only was everything Gil did turning out gold, but we all believed too. Here's how the lefty batters fared against Atlanta:

Lefty Hitter	AVG	G	AB	R	H	HR	RBI
Art Shamsky	.538	3	13	3	7	0	1
Wayne Garrett	.385	3	13	3	5	1	3
Ken Boswell	.333	3	12	4	4	2	5
Ed Kranepool	.250	3	12	2	3	0	1

There was no MVP awarded in the Championship Series until the late 1970s. Who can say which Met the writers in the press box would have picked if there'd been a vote in 1969? I don't think you could have gone wrong choosing from a half dozen Mets: Cleon (.429, 1 HR, 4 RBIs), Agee (.357, 2 HRs, 4 RBIs), Ryan (seven-inning relief stint, pennant-clinching win, 2.57 ERA, 7Ks, 2BBs), Boswell, Garrett, or me. Or give it to all of us together! We didn't care. We were too busy pouring champagne on each other in the locker room at Shea.

Looking Up an Old Friend in Baltimore

Before the first game of the 1969 World Series, we were on the field while the Orioles took batting practice at Memorial Stadium. I caught Frank Robinson's eye and gave him a quick hello from a distance. The day of the World Series opener isn't the time to have an old-school reunion, so we kept it short and professional. That meeting reminded me of the first "real" discussion we had—in the middle of a game in the on-deck circle. It was 1965 in Cincinnati, and Frank was the former (and future) MVP who had been drilled in the arm the day before, and I was the rookie the manager wanted to put in to bat for the All-Star. I'd been in the major leagues for all of just a few weeks; I was so green I was even calling Frank Mr. Robinson. (By the way, my first big league hit was in Chicago against Ted Abernathy, another sidearm pitcher, who came down low. He was called the Worm because his hand almost touched the ground in his motion—digging up worms with his knuckles.)

But back to Frank Robinson: We were playing the Mets in the first game of a doubleheader in early 1965 at Crosley Field. Frank had been hit badly in the arm by a pitch in the previous game, but he insisted on playing. Robby was a tough, hardnosed player who got hit a lot—he stood on top of the plate and didn't give an inch.

We took the lead in the game, and Casey Stengel brought in a sidearming right-handed relief pitcher named Tom Parsons. Frank was the first batter he had to face. Reds manager Dick Sisler called out my name. I was sitting on the bench, minding my own business, not imagining a guy with five career at-bats would be batting for one of baseball's big stars in the middle of a game. "Go hit for Frank," Sisler said to me.

I did one of those "You talking to me?" motions, and then I grabbed a bat as Parsons warmed up. I went out to the on-deck circle, and Frank said, "What the hell are you doing here?" And he didn't say *hell*.

I said, "He wants me to hit for you." Frank then said in so many words, "There's no way."

So I dragged my bat back to the dugout, and Sisler, who unfortunately was a stutterer, had a hard time expressing his disbelief that I had come back. Then he managed to spit out emphatically, "I said go hit for him!"

"He doesn't want me to hit for him."

"I'm the manager. Go back out there!"

I went back out there, and by then the umpire was yelling, "Let's go!"

Sisler, who was having a hard time talking, called out, "Come on, Frank!" He pointed to his arm and added, "You got hit yesterday; your arm is sore. C'mon."

So Frank started to go back to the dugout, stopped, and said to me, "Whatever you do, don't embarrass me." That was all I needed to hear. Now I was in a panic. I said to myself as I went up to the batter's box, "Please, please. If anyone is up there listening, don't let me strike out. Let me hit the first pitch—a pop-up, a ground-out, anything so long as I don't strike out."

So what happened? I hit the first pitch over the center-field wall at Crosley Field pinch-hitting for Frank Robinson. Against the Mets. My first major league home run: May 2, 1965.

I was rounding the bases and I was saying to myself, "Whoever is up there, thank you." Vada Pinson crossed home plate in front of me. We went back in the dugout, and the man

I'd been calling Mr. Robinson since spring training shook my hand and said, "OK, now you can call me Frank."

Paper Tiger

We were a timely hitting team in 1969, but we weren't going to overpower anybody. Our numbers from that year looked somewhat pedestrian, even while platooning at four positions, with left-handed batters against right-handed pitchers and vice versa.

1969 Stat Splits	AVG/OBP/SLUG
LHB vs. RHP	.249/.324/.350
RHB vs. LHP	.241/.320/.368

Three-quarters of the starting pitchers the Mets faced in 1969 were right-handed (120 games vs. 42). All Mets hitters actually batted higher overall against lefties: vs. LHP .238/.302/.360 and vs. RHP .243/.309/.348, though clearly in far fewer at-bats.

That's what was so different about the '69 World Series. The Mets faced right-handed starters three-quarters of the time during the regular season. All three games against the Braves in the NLCS came against righties. Atlanta used two lefties, but they only threw an inning each in relief. Yet four of the five games in the World Series saw the Orioles use left-handed starters.

Baltimore's two left-handed starters, Mike Cuellar and Dave McNally, went 43–18 over 559.1 innings with a 2.78 ERA and 348 strikeouts in 79 combined starts during the season. These southpaws allowed just two earned runs combined in 19 innings in the ALCS against the Twins, with McNally pitching a three-hit shutout over 11 innings before pinch-hitter Curt Motton finally drove home Game 2's only run. The previous day Paul Blair won Game 1 against the Twins with a two-out squeeze bunt in the 12th inning.

And let's not forgot Baltimore's third starter, right-hander Jim Palmer, who would win three Cy Young Awards in the 1970s and eventually ended up in the Hall of Fame. Palmer was just 23 years old and coming off two seasons of being injured, but he went 16–4 with a 3.24 ERA in 23 starts and three relief appearances in 1969, the best winning percentage by a starter in the American League. His one start in the 1969 Championship Series against the Twins was a complete-game victory to clinch the pennant as the Orioles exploded for 11 runs.

Both Palmer and McNally had pitched in the World Series before, with both tossing shutouts against the Dodgers in the 1966 World Series. Most of their team was still intact, with Boog Powell, Davey Johnson, Blair, and both Robinsons having started every game in the 1966 World Series. The Mets' lone World Series veteran was Ron Taylor, who had pitched twice in relief against the Yankees in the 1964 Series.

On paper the 1969 World Series looked like a mismatch. After Game 1, when Don Buford led off with a home run and the Orioles went on to a 4–1 win, it was hard to argue with the critics. Unless you were in our clubhouse. I made the last out pinch-hitting with two outs in the ninth inning off Mike Cuellar. I'm always thankful that Gil had enough confidence to put me up there with the game on the line—against a lefty. Unfortunately, I grounded out to second. That at-bat continues to be a disappointment for me, and I think about it almost every day, even now. Some moments in life never fade from your mind.

Doctor on the Mound

Ron Taylor never got the credit he deserved. In 1969 he pitched well in the playoffs and extremely well in the World Series. When people reflect on the 1969 team, they always say Tug McGraw was the short reliever. Well, we really didn't have one short reliever—we had two. Our starting pitching was so good we didn't usually need that much bullpen help. But when it got late and a reliever was needed, we were glad to have a veteran like Ron Taylor.

The save rule was new in 1969, and there were new requirements for what constituted a "save" for a relief pitcher. Ron pitched twice in the playoffs against Atlanta, didn't allow a run, and won one game and saved another. Whatever definition you want to use, Taylor truly saved us in Game 2 of the World Series in Baltimore.

We were down one game to none and had just taken the lead in the top of the ninth. We really needed to get out of Memorial Stadium with a win. Jerry Koosman got the first two outs in the bottom of the ninth before walking the next two. Gil came out to the mound and signaled for Ron.

Brooks Robinson was due up. He pulled the ball toward third base. Ed Charles made a great play on the ball, grabbed the short hop, and got Brooks at first. We didn't have a lot of veterans, but Ron Taylor and Ed Charles really came through for us. If we lost Game 2, we were liable to lose four in a row, like all the "experts" said before the World Series.

I found Ron to be a fascinating character. He was a working electrical engineer—with a degree from the University of Toronto. Then he decided to go back to school after baseball, and—ready for this?—he became a doctor. He was from

Toronto and served as team physician for the Blue Jays for 36 years. I used to kid him all the time, "I am never going to even let you take my blood pressure. I can't believe you're a doctor." He was very smart—always reading books, always something on his mind.

Ron was the only person on the team with postseason experience since he'd pitched for the Cardinals in the 1964 World Series when they beat the Yankees. He was a sinker-slider pitcher. No tricks, and he basically had two pitches: a fastball that went down on the batter, and a slider. We nicknamed him the Duke, though I have no idea why we called him that. What we thought of him, though, was that he was reliable and cool under pressure.

Close-Up View of an Amazin' Catch

I was right next to Tommie Agee when he made his second great catch in Game 2 of the World Series, sprawling on his stomach on the warning track in right-center to strand the bases loaded on Paul Blair's drive in the seventh. There's a picture of me running behind Tommie, backing up in case he didn't make the catch. Blair could fly, and he was sure to clear the bases and get at least a triple if the ball hadn't been caught. In the picture are three guys standing on a platform above the fence and under the Rheingold sign attached to the bottom of the scoreboard—they may have been the only people who had a better view of the play than I did. I used to tease Tommie all the time about making an easy play look hard.

His incredible catch—like the one he'd made in the fourth inning—was the third out of the inning. As we ran toward the dugout and the crowd at Shea was screaming, it flashed through my mind really quickly that you dream about having the kind of day like Tommie had in the World Series. He had already hit a home run leading off the bottom of the first—the first Met to bat in a World Series game in New York, and he drilled it out of the park. And then he came up with a catch like that in the World Series—twice! He saved five, maybe six runs. That's what I was thinking about as I was running in off the field.

They say you make a great play and you lead off the next inning—and Tommie did. Announcer Curt Gowdy even said it as the crowd roared as he led off the bottom of the seventh. The Orioles walked him. I guess they'd finally figured out it was just his day and to stay away from him.

Nolan Ryan, Part II

I've said this before, but the essence of how Gil handled the team was by feel. There was no statistical report that he looked at. I don't think you can look at a stat sheet and say, "Well, here's a tight situation in Game 3—I'm going to bring Nolan Ryan in." The young and wild Nolan Ryan we had? He wouldn't have been your first choice. But in each game—the first Championship Series and then the first World Series ever played at Shea—there was Ryan. In both cases he came in for Gary Gentry with the game on the line.

It worked out pretty well against the Braves in the NLCS, so he went back to it eight days later in the World Series. Gentry was pitching great against the Orioles in Game 3, but in the seventh, he ran out of gas. He walked the bases loaded, and Gil went to the mound. Ryan rode in on the little bullpen cart again. Three men on base and Paul Blair representing the tying run. Blair crushed the fastball, and Tommie Agee made that second sprawling catch. Ryan went the rest of the way, and we took the lead in the Series.

Two games with tough situations at crucial parts of the games, and Gil brought in Nolan both times. He went 9.1 innings in relief combined and got the win in one game and the save in the second. In a career that lasted 27 seasons, Nolan had just three saves. And Gil brought him in twice in a week out of the bullpen in the biggest games the Mets had played to that point in their history. And that was Nolan's only World Series appearance in his very long and illustrious career.

Everyone Involved

In the long term, platooning had an effect on some of us in terms of our careers. In negotiations with management, we were always told we didn't play enough to be paid more than they wanted to pay. When we landed on other teams, which happens to the vast majority of players during their career, managers didn't think of us as everyday players. But in 1969 it worked for the Mets. Man, did it work.

One of the trademarks of Gil Hodges as a manager was that he got everyone on the roster involved. Nobody felt like they weren't part of the team or that they never got a chance. He played everybody: Bobby Pfeil, Duffy Dyer, J. C. Martin, and Rod Gaspar. Rod made the team out of spring training because I got hurt. He's always thanking me for that. Here are some other interesting facts: Even Amos Otis, who was brought up and down from the minors several times and was a very unwilling participant in Gil's third-base experiment, played 35 (errorless) games in the outfield. Amos only hit .151, but he still had more than 100 plate appearances. Seventeen Mets came to the plate 100 or more times in 1969, with Duffy missing that number mostly because he was the third-string rookie catcher while Grote and Martin were experts at handling the staff.

People look at Gil Hodges as someone who pulled the right strings. His ability to get everyone involved was one of the key reasons we won in the long run. In so many games, unsung heroes were coming through. Four guys who weren't very well-known at the time came through for us in the World Series: Al Weis, Nolan Ryan, J. C. Martin, and Rod Gaspar. Gaspar and Martin had their moments of fame on the same play: a bunt that Gil called and they executed!

Over the past 50-plus years, when people mention the 1969 Mets, they don't just mention Seaver, Jones, Agee, Koosman, Clendenon—the usual people; they mention all those other names who contributed to that season. I think that is the true legacy of that team.

Swoboda's Catch and Martin's Bunt

I saw Tom Seaver pitch plenty of incredible games, but his Game 4 effort at Shea in the 1969 Series was about the best I ever saw, especially with a world championship at stake. He allowed only one run, but the play that scored the run is unforgettable.

We were clinging to a 1–0 lead in the ninth, but the Orioles had first and third with nobody out with Brooks Robinson at the plate. Since the Orioles started a left-handed pitcher, Mike Cuellar, Ron Swoboda got the start in right field. Ron wasn't known as a great defensive outfielder, but he had been working on his defense all year and was ready at the crack of the bat. I asked Ronnie about it, and this is what he told me: "I anticipated the possibility of a fly ball coming my way. There was a runner on third, so I was thinking about the situation—that if a fly ball came my way, I'd try and make the throw home. As it turned out, when Brooks Robinson hit the ball toward right field, I just reacted and made the diving catch and then still tried to make the throw home. Really, I just reacted. I love that people still talk about that play."

Frank Robinson tagged up and scored, but the catch cut off Baltimore's rally. The game went to the 10th inning tied, and Orioles left fielder Don Buford misjudged a fly ball and Jerry Grote reached second. Baltimore walked Al Weis, and lefty Pete Richert came in to face pinch-hitter J. C. Martin. He laid down a bunt, Richert picked up the ball, and the throw glanced off J. C. running to first base. The ball bounced away while pinch-runner Rod Gaspar scored the winning run. That's the biggest moment in both J. C. and Rod's careers. They were both heroes—on a bunt! That's a moment in New York sports history that will never be forgotten.

J. C. and his wife, Barbara, were married 67 years. She passed while I was writing this. When I talked to J. C., I wanted to reassure him that he was such an integral part of that team. We talk about Jerry Grote as the great defensive catcher, but J. C. played a lot and had some very good games—as did Duffy Dyer, who was a rookie in '69 and went on to have a long career and ended up managing in the minors.

I hear about it all the time when I do appearances. There's always an event or moment or two during that season that fans focus on, whether they were there or not. That bunt is one of them. Topps even put out a baseball card the following year with a picture of that perfect bunt. The card says: "Martin's bunt ends deadlock!" It was unforgettable for anyone who was watching. And it's unbelievable how many Mets fans who were born decades later know it as well as if they had been there. They were there in their minds. That's one of the Amazin' things about that team and that magical year.

Polishing Off the Birds

We did not want to go back to Baltimore. And though we had a lead of three games to one, we all remembered the previous year's World Series, in which Detroit faced elimination and won the last three games against St. Louis. In Game 7 the best center fielder in the National League misjudged a fly ball that opened the door for the Tigers—I'd never seen Curt Flood not reel in a catchable ball. Anything can happen in the World Series.

During Game 5 against the Orioles, I was in the dugout thinking, *We've gotten a lot of breaks this year, and we have to take advantage once more.* Man, did we catch one more break.

Down 3–0 in the sixth inning, a pitch in the dirt bounced into the Mets dugout. The umpire, Lou DiMuro, said the ball didn't hit Cleon—just as he'd insisted an inside pitch didn't hit Frank Robinson earlier in the inning. I saw the whole thing unfold like everyone else, though I was at the other end of the dugout from where Gil was sitting. He emerged with a ball with a smudge of shoe polish on it. That was all the proof the umpire needed. Cleon was sent to first. Donn Clendenon followed with a home run. Al Weis hit a game-tying home run an inning later.

Ron Swoboda hit a tiebreaking double off right-hander Eddie Watt in the eighth. Like I've said before, Gil was predictably unpredictable. Regardless of the stakes, he was not afraid to go with his gut instead of with the platoon or "the book." A lot of things certainly went our way in 1969. Tom Seaver was correct when he said God was a Mets fan.

Run for Your Life!

There's that moment when you see what's going to happen: the ball is in the air, on its way into the glove, and you know you're going to win—the division, the pennant, the world championship. And then the hordes descend.

Even when the fans storm the field for the third time in four weeks, it's a little frightening because you don't know what's going to happen. To be truthful, if people started pouring out of the stands today, I'd really be scared because of the world we live in. Back then it was just fans' excitement about where we'd come from and where we were at that moment. All three of those celebrations were at Shea. Fans always seemed to run on to the field when their team won something in the 1960s. It was the first year of divisional play, so we had an extra reason to celebrate: clinching the NL East title. Come one, come all!

You're running for your life after you celebrate on the field with your teammates—if you can get there because of this throng of people. It's not scary so much as it is discombobulating. Once we got past the dugout and into the clubhouse, there was security. On the field was mayhem—everyone was so caught up in it.

The locker room was almost as crazy. While the champagne was being poured and the beer was flying, it occurred to me that right outside the locker room were friends and relatives waiting near the elevator that led to the Diamond Club, the restaurant on the press level at Shea. At that moment I thought it would be nice to bring my dad into the locker room to witness it for himself. I stuck my head outside the door amid all the yelling, and I saw my father. I motioned for him to come on in.

The first few steps into the clubhouse, I think he was amazed at what was going on. Victory celebrations are always wild, and there was no protective covering from champagne or anything, no glasses or ski goggles to shield your eyes from being stung by the bubbly. It was just a wild scene, and my dad was amazed I'd brought him in. My father and I at times had some, let's say, overbearing moments—as happens with many fathers and sons. He was the one who got me started in baseball and closely followed every game I played. I thought it was nice for him to see this accomplishment, what we'd achieved as a team. I never told anyone, but I am really glad I did that.

Parade

The parade was another incredible day. The number of people in attendance and the blizzard of confetti (58 tons, writer Wayne Coffey reported) raining down on us set records for the city, but I'll never forget the love for the team that was so abundantly on display. The Jets had not gotten a ticker-tape parade after winning the Super Bowl in January, and the Knicks would not have a parade but instead a celebration with Mayor John Lindsay when they won the NBA title the following spring.

I rode in the same car as Ken Boswell down the Canyon of Heroes. It seemed an easy call for the Mets to just put roommates together in the cars as we headed down Broadway. Being in front of all those people is hard to explain. You can't hear anything and you're constantly getting hit with confetti. You just try to take in an event you'll always remember—let it wash all over you.

The parade was the culmination of so many things. We'd cut an album already. The night before the parade we'd been on *The Ed Sullivan Show* so we could plug our new release—like any big-shot entertainer! These appearances and adulation were a prelude to all the things we'd do for years to come based upon what we did that fall as a team.

For me, it was my second year in New York. We barely finished out of 10th place in the National League in 1968, and then a year later we came from 10 games back to overtake the Cubs. It was different for me than for guys such as Eddie Kranepool, Ron Swoboda, Cleon Jones, and Tug McGraw—guys who had been there for the really terrible years. We were all caught up in it, but those guys had seen the good, the bad, and the ugly. That had to be especially exhilarating. I was only there a year before we won, and it will always remain with me.

I never looked at myself as being part of the Lovable Losers, even after my first season there in '68. I just thought of us as the same old Mets. That's the first thing I thought of when I heard the Reds had traded me to the Mets. But I knew things were going to change with Gil Hodges there. I knew things were going to be different. Gil was adamant about being professional. He was adamant about doing things right. He gained the respect of everybody during that first year. I knew things were going to change at Shea. Winning a pennant or a World Series? That was a different story. No one saw that coming, but everyone sure was happy about it!

The fans went wild because they were as eager as the team was to shed that label of Lovable Losers. You could just call us world champions.

The Vegas Mets

Once in a while Kenny Boswell and I would sneak over to Las Vegas after a day game in Los Angeles or San Francisco. If we had a day game or day off and didn't have a game until the next night, we'd fly there. We did that maybe three times. We made friends and met new people. Even though we knew it was risky, it was fun, and we just did it. I tell that story now because, after all, these are stories I tell my friends. As far as Las Vegas, I never imagined there would be a time I would get paid to be there.

After we won the World Series, seven of us were asked to appear at Caesars Palace in Vegas. We got there and rehearsed for three days, and then we did two shows every night for two weeks. We wore tuxedos for the dinner show and casual clothes for the midnight show. What a fantastic time. It turned out to be 17 incredible days. It truly was a once-in-a-lifetime experience!

I'm not sure how they picked the seven of us, but it was Seaver, Koosman, Kranepool, Jones, Agee, Clendenon, and me. We were treated royally.

They paid us each $10,000 for the 17 days. They wouldn't let us withdraw more than $1,000 per week because they didn't want us to lose the money gambling. I can only speak for myself about that—maybe the other guys talked Caesars into letting them withdraw more. The $10,000 was more than 50 percent of what I was making for the season in 1969.

They set us up in junior suites, and we could sign for whatever we wanted. We had our names on the big marquee, but we weren't the only ones on the bill. Country singer Jimmie Rodgers was the headliner. Also performing was Jerry Van Dyke, Dick Van Dyke's younger brother. Comedian Phil Foster served as emcee and had a little banter with each of us. Then we sang "The Impossible Dream."

Caesars Palace was one of the most famous hotel casinos on the strip at the time, and they were really protective of us. One time I was playing blackjack at a table—just the dealer and me. I'm not a big gambler, so it was a five-dollar table.

One of the pit bosses walked over to our table and he looked at my hand, which was open. I had 15. The dealer had two cards I couldn't see. The pit boss looked at the dealer's cards, looked at my cards, and said, "Let's call this hand a draw." He didn't let the dealer draw because he didn't want me to lose that hand. He was a baseball fan or a Mets fan, or maybe he was just watching out for us. Any way you look at it, that's not the way most people are treated at the tables in Vegas.

One night we were performing and Dodgers shortstop Maury Wills was in the audience. We called him up to sing with us. He had no idea and didn't know the words. That was OK. Even after two weeks doing two shows a night, some of us still didn't know all the words.

"While we rehearsed for three days, I'm not sure we all knew the words to the song 'The Impossible Dream,'" Cleon Jones said. "And I knew the words to the song, but I'm not sure the rest of the guys did. During rehearsals they put one or two professional singers behind a curtain to make us sound better, but it didn't make a difference. The audience loved us no matter what."

I'll never forget hearing Donn Clendenon's name every five minutes or so over the hotel's paging system. I know for a fact he was paging himself.

We met so many stars there in those couple of weeks. The great heavyweight boxing champ Joe Louis was working for the hotel. We also met stars including Redd Foxx, Buddy Hackett, Dean Martin, Frank Sinatra, and Elvis Presley in the flesh, among many others. What a wonderful time. We were on such a high.

Tom Seaver ended up leaving early. Jerry Koosman did too, because of the birth of one of his children. He told me that the night before he left he met one of the owners of the Las

Vegas Cowboys, who were part of the Continental Football League. The owner asked Jerry to throw the dice for him at the craps table. Jerry was as hot at the table as he'd been for the Mets in October. It turned out to be a great night for both of them, and Jerry went home with several thousand dollars as part of the winnings. He took those winnings, along with his World Series share and the money he got for performing in Las Vegas, and bought a house for his growing family.

Caesars was always entertaining high rollers, so they were constantly inviting us to banquets and corporate events. What was so much fun was that between our shows, we could go out and see other shows.

We sold out shows almost every night at Caesars Palace, where the biggest stars in Hollywood performed. I don't really think I appreciated it as much then as I do now, remembering it.

Ed Kranepool once told me they wanted us to do another week, but we didn't want to do it. I don't remember that. Oh, I definitely would have stayed. You can't be any more on top of the world than where we were at that time!

Shea's Forgotten Tenants

We were doing so well in 1969, we almost forgot about the world championship football team sharing the stadium with us. The Jets got the short end of the stick and did not play at Shea until our season was over. Of course, the 1969 American Football League schedule maker didn't expect the Mets to be playing in October, so the Jets were scheduled to play at Shea for much of the month. Once we made the playoffs, the Jets were shipped out of town for not one game but two. Luckily for them, they played the Boston Patriots and Cincinnati Bengals twice apiece that year, so the AFL swapped their home and away dates.

The Jets didn't play their first game at Shea until after we had clinched the world championship and had our parade. Then they played all seven home games in as many weeks before going back on the road to win their last two and clinch their second straight division title. The 10–4 Jets lost a playoff game at Shea to the eventual AFL- and Super Bowl–champion Kansas City Chiefs the Saturday before Christmas in 1969. The Jets wouldn't play another playoff game at Shea until 1981. They did a lot of waiting at Shea.

Sharing the stadium with them, we'd see them on occasion at Shea. There was always some event we had to go to, and once in a while those guys were there too: Gerry Philbin, John Elliott, Randy Rasmussen, and sometimes even Joe Namath (but he was already a huge star, so he wasn't available to do things such as open shopping centers off the Jericho Turnpike). The Mets and Jets ended up doing a lot of appearances together, especially on Long Island, where both teams were based.

Over the years we had to listen to the Jets complain about field conditions and the delays in opening their season at Shea, but I think they were happy for us when we won. And we all started to be good friends with each other, and with the Knicks. When I moved into the city, I got to know a lot of the Knicks even better. I spent time with Clyde Frazier, Willis Reed, and Dave DeBusschere. I had played against Dave in the minor leagues when he was a pitching prospect with the White Sox. He broke in with Chicago at the same time his NBA career started with the Detroit Pistons.

One Game the '69 Mets Lost: *The Dating Game*

Now, before I go into this story, I want to be clear that I was married and was not asked to be a contestant in this low point of TV culture that first aired the winter after we won the World Series. You can still watch it on YouTube if you must, but it's not pretty.

For those unfamiliar with *The Dating Game* concept, it was a game show created by Chuck Barris, who today is best remembered for hosting *The Gong Show*. Barris worked for ABC and told the network that the daytime programming they were putting out was worse than his own ideas; they told him he if he knew so much, he should produce his own shows, and that's what he did. His first hit was *The Dating Game*, which premiered in 1965. The show was recorded in front of a studio audience as three bachelors sat onstage (hidden by a screen) while a young woman asked them questions, picked the best one based on their answers, and the new couple was sent on a date to an exotic location—complete with a chaperone!

Just weeks after we won the World Series, the Mets were in demand, and *The Dating Game* landed a trio of bachelors fresh off the baseball pinnacle and without a clue. One was my roommate; for the purposes of the show, he was Bachelor No. 1. Here's the lineup:

1. Ken Boswell
2. Wayne Garrett
3. Rod Gaspar

Lynette Marvin was the unfortunate young woman who had to navigate this unenviable choice. Like many men in the late

1960s, all three Mets had sideburns—and not an interesting thing to say.

The segment started with a clip of Cleon Jones catching the final out of the World Series. Host Jim Lange commented that the win "led to one of the most hysterical love-ins in sports history." You could have turned your sets off there—and you should have. The questions the bachelorette tossed at the bachelors were softballs, and the best these three could do was foul them off.

The bachelors each received a black-and-white television set for appearing on the show. They got a TV for embarrassing themselves on TV! The winning bachelor—Rod Gaspar—and his date received a ski trip to Switzerland. That was an ironic choice by the producers, because major league players all had it written in their contracts that they couldn't ski because Boston's Cy Young winner Jim Lonborg had messed up his knee skiing following the 1967 season.

I never let Boswell or Garrett forget that Gaspar was picked. Rod didn't have a whole lot of personality, and he beat Garrett and Boswell, who together couldn't make one personality! I always tell Rod that when the woman came around the screen and saw he was the one she had picked, she must have freaked out. I later made about 10 copies of that episode and gave them to friends of mine. It's one of those classic shows that I look at and laugh at all the time.

The Dating Game was only part of what happened to *all* of us after we won the World Series. Ron Swoboda and I were on *The Dick Cavett Show*, hitting against a fast-pitch softball pitcher. She threw it right by me; Swoboda was able to foul off a pitch. Cavett interviewed us too—along with Ed Kranepool, Ron Taylor, and Jerry Koosman.

Another one of my favorite 1969 Mets experiences was being on *Sesame Street*. The kids counted as Kranepool and I took turns throwing and swinging. We did 1 to 10 and 11 to 20. I don't recall how many kids were there, but it was a lot of fun. It was early in the program's run, and the production wasn't that sophisticated compared to what it is now. I'm just glad no fast-pitch pitcher came out and started firing at us.

Chapter 5

A TOUGH ACT
TO FOLLOW

Talking to Gil Hodges

When I go out and speak at events and make appearances, I run into a lot of old Brooklyn Dodgers fans or Mets fans from the 1960s. They almost always ask the same thing: "How was Gil Hodges to play for?"

Gil was a tough, stern disciplinarian. Yet he managed by feel. He got everybody on the team involved. Sure, he platooned regularly, but he moved people in and out of the lineup all the time. Just be ready to play no matter who is pitching. And you basically knew when he wanted you to come off the bench without him even speaking. I think I almost got to the point where I could predict what he was going to do, particularly when it came to me. You just knew you had to be prepared.

Our entire Mets careers coincided. We both arrived at Shea Stadium to start the 1968 season and I was there when Gil managed his last regular-season game in 1971. In all that time I really only had three direct, face-to-face conversations with him.

1.) The only time I recall having a conversation with him on the bench during a game was in Atlanta. I am pretty sure it was 1968. I was playing left field against the Braves and there was a ground-ball single to left field and the Braves runner went from first to third base, which is something that should never happen. I don't remember who was running, but it wasn't like there were two outs or a full count or the runner was stealing and kept going to third. When the inning was over, Gil stood up and called me over to sit down next to him. I knew that I was in a little bit of trouble. And he said, very simply, "I don't ever want to see a runner go from first to third on single to left field." That's all he said to me. I said, "You're right." There was nothing more that I could say and that was the end of it. I had that in the back of my mind every time I played left field for the Mets after that. I don't recall anyone going from first to third on me in left field again—or there would have an even more difficult conversation.

2.) The next time was the conversation with him and Johnny Murphy right after I came off the disabled list at the start of the season in 1969, which I wrote about earlier in the book. To summarize, this was not my finest moment, but it turned into my greatest year.

3.) The third was the brief conversation I had with him talking about my taking off for a Jewish holiday in 1969, which I also discussed earlier in the book. It still amazes me how calm Gil was and the way he made me feel that whatever decision I made was fine. When you have created a team where everybody is ready to play at any time, you are not surprised—you are always prepared.

Basically, that was it in terms of one-on-one conversations with Gil.

He congratulated everyone personally after the World Series victory, but it wasn't really a conversation. He just said a word or two and went on to the next person. We were all caught up in that frenzy of the locker room celebration with champagne and shaving cream. We always seemed to be in groups during those moments, showering each other with champagne and celebrating.

Gil was not really the type of person who would slap you on the back when you did something well or chastise you when you screwed up. He was very level-headed. My relationship was at arm's length. I had total respect for him as a manager because he was fair. I didn't need him to be someone I had to see after every 0-for-4.

Other than the times he hit ground balls to me and said a word or two, those three times were the extent of my conversations with Gil. But there was another situation that would certainly have led to our fourth conversation if he had found out what went on one night on a road trip with his son, Gil Jr., who was then a teenager.

Gil Jr.'s Beach Party

On a road trip to the West Coast, Gil's son, Gil Jr., made the trip with the team. I believe he was 19. Before a Saturday day game in Los Angeles, I was standing near the batting cage. Ken Boyer was playing for the Dodgers at the time. Remember the fraternizing rules? Despite them, Ken found me before the game. He talked quickly: "Some friends are having a party at the beach later. If you want to go, I'll send the address over to the locker room."

I got the address, and Kenny Boswell and I went back to the hotel after the game to get ready. Gilly, which was what we usually called Gil Jr., was sitting near us on the bus back to the hotel, and we asked him if he'd like to go. (Gil Jr. didn't like sitting on the bus with his dad, who always sat up front with pitching coach Rube Walker.) Even as we were talking to Gilly about the party, we knew we shouldn't be asking him if he wanted to go, for obvious reasons. But we did anyway. I guess we liked to live dangerously!

We had a curfew of midnight because there was an afternoon game the next day. In this case, we were not as concerned about the curfew as we were about Gil's son going with us. We mentioned this to him, but he wanted to go, so we made arrangements. The party was on the beach—I don't remember which one. In Los Angeles you need a car to get anywhere, and that included us getting to the party from our hotel. Kenny rented a car. It was one of the first times he actually spent some money.

The three of us went to this party, and there were a lot of people there. Around 11:00 PM Gil Jr. came over and asked us about the curfew. I said, "Come back in 15 minutes and we'll leave." But he must've met someone to hang out with, and he didn't come back for more than two hours. When we saw Gil Jr. again, he asked, "Don't you guys have a curfew?" We told him he was supposed to have come back and gotten us. He said, "I was busy." We just gave him the keys to the rental car, telling him, "We're already out, and we're already in trouble if we get caught, so what difference does it make what time we get back?" Kenny and I figured we'd get a ride to the hotel.

To this day—and I talked to him about it recently—Gil Jr. still doesn't know how he found the hotel. He wasn't drunk or anything like that, but he was pretty young, and he was driving around L.A. at night with no GPS to guide him. Well, he got to the hotel at around 2:30 AM and went up to the room he was sharing with his dad, who was sleeping. He didn't wake up Gil Sr., but at about 3:00 in the morning the phone rang, and Gil Sr. answered it. Somebody from the hotel staff said, "You need to move your car that you just parked." Gil Sr. hung and said to Gil Jr., "What car? You don't have a car. Go take care of this and see what the problem is."

Gilly went down to move the car and then went back to bed. His dad never said anything about the car, but the next day he had a conversation with Gil Jr. about the situation. He said, "I know you were with some players last night. I don't want to know who they were, but I never want you going out with any players again!"

When it was all said and done, Kenny and I were very fortunate how it worked out. If Gil knew it was us who had brought Gilly to a party, we would have been in big trouble. I never spoke about this or wrote about it while Gil Sr. or his wife, Joan, was alive. She died in 2022, a few months after Gil finally was inducted into the Hall of Fame.

I called up Gil Jr., and we decided: Why not tell the story now? What difference does it make? They can't fine me—I think it's a little too late for that. Gilly's not going to get in trouble. I think waiting to tell the story until now goes a long way toward our respect for—and fear of—Gil as a manager. We never talked about it to anyone else. And there have been no shortage of stories about those years—from me and just about everyone else on the '69 team. Kenny and I did kid around with Gil Jr. about it over the years, but that was it. In the long run, we were really lucky Gil never found out it was us. If he had, I think he would have fined us pretty heavily, or worse, he would have gotten rid of us altogether. (As for

Kenny and me, we aren't sure how we got back to the hotel. We just don't remember.)

There were many nights we stayed out a bit late when a righty would be pitching against us the next day, which meant Kenny and I would be in the starting lineup. We somehow got through it. It basically came down to just using common sense—at least most of the time.

Again, I had the utmost respect for Gil Hodges as a manager and a person. I never saw him say no to autographs. I never saw him have many arguments with umpires. I don't recall him ever being thrown out of a game. I looked it up, and he was never tossed by an umpire in more than 2,000 games as a player. As a manager he was ejected seven times, but not once in 1969.

Tug

I loved being around Frank "Tug" McGraw. He was one of those guys—and Ron Swoboda was a little like this too—who would say anything at any time to anyone. You always had to be on your toes around him, because you never knew what he was going to say and how you were going to react. He's famous for the "Ya Gotta Believe" rally cry in 1973, an off-the-cuff line that everyone picked up on as the Mets went from last place to first place in the span of a month and beat the Big Red Machine for the pennant.

I was no longer a Met by 1973, but I was sitting not far from him in the Candlestick Park locker room in San Francisco a couple years earlier when he uttered one of his most famous lines after a game against the Giants. Candlestick Park experimented with artificial turf in the early 1970s, and after a game he pitched there, Tug was asked what the difference was between AstroTurf and natural grass. Without batting an eye,

How can you not be happy when you're in uniform in a major league dugout?

Tommie Agee makes his second great catch in Game 3 of the 1969 World Series, while I back up the play. I always kidded, "You sure know how to make an easy catch look hard."
AP Images

Just about every member of that 1969 team feels like a brother to me. *AP Images*

Tom Seaver was a leader on the field and off it. He had great physical skill, a keen competitive edge, and could outthink and outwork opponents. *AP Images*

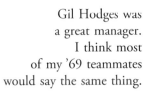

Gil Hodges was a great manager. I think most of my '69 teammates would say the same thing.

Art Baumgarten's Major League All-Stars was a team of baseball players who played basketball around New York between the 1968 and '69 seasons. Pictured (left to right) are Baumgarten, Jack Lamabe, Bill Robinson, Ed Kranepool, me, Jeff Torborg, Al Jackson, and Bill Monbouquette.

You know the old joke about how to get to Carnegie Hall: practice, practice, practice. But nobody ever said *baseball* practice.

Here we are at Tommie Agee's wedding in 1985. Just like our 1969 outfield, Cleon Jones is on the left, Tommie (with Maxcine) in center, and me on the right.

I posed for the cover of *Bazaar* magazine in 1970 with iconic model Lauren Hutton.

I briefly tried my hand at modeling and acting in (you guessed it) the 1970s.

Just after the 1969 World Series, Tug McGraw (with friends) helped open The Marshmallow—the restaurant owned by former Met and Yankee Phil Linz and me in Rockland County, New York.

I have worked in some capacity for many media outlets, from the early days of cable TV to being an original host at WFAN to interviewing a young Zack Wheeler (left) for WPIX-TV. You can see my World Series ring, which he tried on, dangling off his right pinkie.

Archbishop of New York Cardinal Timothy Dolan and I both hail from St. Louis. We struck up a good relationship that began with our shared adulation of Stan "the Man" Musial and the 1960s Cardinals.

Here I am signing autographs before a game I managed in the Israeli Baseball League in 2007.

Above is one of the balls we used. All I can make out is the signature of Daniel Kurtzer, IBL commissioner and former US ambassador to Israel and Egypt.

Mets owner Steve Cohen is determined to win a world championship.

Ed Kranepool was unable to address transplant donors and recipients at St. Patrick's Cathedral, so I was honored to step in for my good friend.

Johnny Bench and I go back to our days in Cincinnati in the 1960s. We met up at the dedication of the Freedom class combat ship USS *Cooperstown* in New York in 2023.

The producer of *Everybody Loves Raymond* was a big fan of mine and named the dog on the show Shamsky. A number of 1969 Mets appeared in an episode of the show, including (left to right) Bud Harrelson and Ed Kranepool (with Ron Swoboda signing a baseball behind me), alongside star Ray Romano and his real-life son.

Once a Met, always a Met. *AP Images*

he said, "I don't know. I never smoked AstroTurf." The way he said that without a pause was one of the most amazing things I've ever heard.

Another great line he tossed off is more of a motto than a one-liner: "Ten million years from now, when then sun burns out and the Earth is just a frozen iceball hurtling through space, nobody's going to care whether or not I got this guy out." That sums up Tug's attitude toward those pressure-packed situations a reliever can find himself in several times per week. When the other team beats you in their last at-bat, trust me, you will be annoyed after the game. Come the next day, though, you have to go out there again, forget what happened yesterday, and get this guy out—even if no one will remember it in 10 million years.

One of my favorite Tug moments occurred in a game that really didn't matter. It was a spring training B game, which always started in the morning. Usually the guys who played the B game were not scheduled to play in the main game in the afternoon. It was mostly to simulate in-game situations against another team trying to get their work in. There was hardly anybody in the stands at B games, except maybe a cleanup crew trying to get *their* work in. This game was at Huggins-Stengel Field, and I was playing first base, so I had a good view of Tug when he decided it was time for a little fun in the middle of all that work.

Few people knew that Tug was ambidextrous. He could bat and throw right as well as left—he batted righty in games and was very proud of his hitting. He batted a lot for us because when we went into extra innings, no one wanted to take him out in a game that was still undecided. He was a different breed of reliever than you'll see today—most of the games he relieved in, he pitched more than one inning; his average outing lasted five outs. Tug pitched six innings in Game 2 of the 1973 World Series—in relief! Today announcers get all worked up if a *starter* goes six innings.

Sure, Tug's left arm was durable, but he could throw right-handed too. And in this spring training B game, he was pitching to get some work in. The first batter was a switch-hitter who was batting right. So Tug suddenly decided he was going to throw right-handed. He moved his glove to the other hand, and the batter decided that if Tug was going to pitch right-handed, he was going to bat left-handed, like he usually did against righties. Then Tug switched back to being a lefty. And the batter hopped on the other side of the batter's box. They went back and forth for about a minute while we were trying not to crack up in the field.

Finally our pitching coach, Rube Walker, went out. Tug was an established major leaguer, and Rube just wanted him to get his throwing in. I went over to the mound for the conference, and Rube said to him, "Tug, what do you want to be today? Right-handed or left-handed? We don't care. Whatever it is, just decide."

Of course, Tug went back to being a southpaw that morning. With Tug McGraw, the only assumption was that there was no one else you wanted on the mound with the game on the line.

How *Bazaar*: On the Cover with Lauren Hutton

My fashion magazine debut will give you an idea of how crazy things got in the aftermath of the 1969 postseason. I not only was on the cover of *Harper's Bazaar*, America's first fashion magazine (dating back to 1867), but I beat out several all-time sports figures to do it. The May 1970 issue of *Harper's Bazaar* was dubbed the "Sports Heroes & Fashion Winners" issue. Given what Donn Clendenon had already told me about my fashion sense, it was probably a good thing they just had me bring my Mets uniform to the shoot.

Athletes in the magazine for the May 1970 issue were all among the top stars in their respective sports: Mark Spitz (Olympic gold medal swimmer), Willie Shoemaker (Triple Crown jockey), Terry Bradshaw (up-and-coming star quarterback), Arthur Ashe (groundbreaking tennis champion), and Mario Andretti (1969 Indianapolis 500 winner and legendary driver). The editors of *Harper's Bazaar* could have used any one of those big-name people for the cover, but they picked me. It really was the Mets' year.

Though the photo shoot took place in the winter, the magazine made me look tan and put makeup on me. World-class model Lauren Hutton was on the cover of *Vogue* 26 times, a record. And there she was preparing for one of the eight times she was on the cover of *Harper's Bazaar*, and I was taking photos with her. I was told early on that no male had ever been on the cover of the US version of *Harper's Bazaar*, but a little research showed that Steve McQueen, Warren Beatty, and Dustin Hoffman all beat me to it by a couple of years. But I was the magazine's first male cover athlete. I look at that cover and wish I looked like that now!

Charles to Otis to Foy

I think the first trade the Mets made after winning the 1969 World Series was a mistake. The Mets let Ed Charles go after we won the 1969 world championship and replaced him at third base with Joe Foy. Joe was a good guy. There are stories that he got involved in drugs. I don't know for a fact what he was doing, and I don't want to disparage him, but at times he looked like he was in another world.

The Mets got Joe from the Royals for Amos Otis a few weeks after the '69 World Series. Amos went on to be a great hitter and Gold Glove center fielder with Kansas City. The Mets wanted Amos to play third base, a position he did not want to play. That was not going to work. As good as some of the trades the Mets made leading up to '69 were, in addition to getting Donn Clendenon in the middle of the season, Amos Otis for Joe Foy was not a good trade at all.

I think the Mets at that time forgot how important Ed Charles was to the team. He was a terrific player, but just as important, he was the glue in the clubhouse. The Glider, as he was nicknamed, was the calming antithesis to the havoc Clendenon created. Ed had gone through the awful period earlier when he was not able to get to the majors because of the color of his skin. He understood life's ups and downs and was able to pass on his wonderful words of wisdom to others. In my mind, he was invaluable, and at least he finished his career on top after the 1969 championship.

Marked Mets in '70

After the 1969 season, we weren't going to sneak up on anybody. As long as you have pitching and defense, you're going to have a chance. You generally win games with pitching and defense. We had plenty of both in 1970, but I don't know why we didn't win.

The Pirates pulled away from us down the stretch. One difference from a year earlier was that we were 24–27 in one-run games and 9–11 in extra innings. In 1969 we thrived in those situations (41–23, 10–6), and we had so many dramatic late wins. Maybe it was the relief pitching, or perhaps we didn't have the timely hitting in '70. We led the majors in ERA (3.45) and strikeouts (1,064), plus Tom Seaver had another excellent season.

I had a pretty good year. I was hitting .328 when the first half of the season ended and thought I had a chance to make the All-Star team. I was going to beat out Willie Mays? Hank Aaron? Roberto Clemente? Pete Rose? Lou Brock, Billy Williams, and Willie Stargell didn't even make the team as reserves. I had no shot. Starting left fielder Rico Carty was hitting almost 40 points higher than me. There was no way I was making the cut—even with my manager deciding on the All-Star selections that year (because he'd managed the team that won the previous World Series). I had a good year and led the team in hitting (.293).

We did not repeat in 1970 because guys didn't have the same kind of year. We also had some young players break in that year. Ken Singleton was a big, strong kid. He ended up having some really good years in Baltimore later on. Mike Jorgensen grew up in Queens and went to Bayside High. He was one of those guys who if you said he'd one day be an executive in baseball, I'd have said you were crazy. He became farm director for the Cardinals and even managed that team for a while. I didn't foresee that for him as a 21-year-old first baseman with the Mets.

There were a number of good teams in the National League East. After 1969 the Pirates dominated the division, winning NL East titles in 1970, '71, '72, '74, and '75, and they put together another great team at the end of the decade to win their second World Series in nine years over the Baltimore Orioles.

The 1970 Pirates had Willie Stargell and Roberto Clemente—plus they were constantly coming up with good young players: Manny Sanguillen, Al Oliver, Richie Hebner, Freddie Patek, Dock Ellis, Steve Blass, and Bob Moose, who already had a no-hitter against us and was only 22. The Pirates always had a good lineup, earning the nickname the Pittsburgh Lumber Company. Stargell just killed the Mets. He hit the first home run at Shea when it opened in 1964, and he hit the first Pirates homer at Three Rivers Stadium when it opened in 1970. Willie hit the first ball into the upper deck in Pittsburgh against Ron Taylor a few weeks after the stadium opened, which I witnessed. I think it broke a seat out there. I always reminded Ron Taylor about that Stargell home run.

We managed to tie the Pirates for first place on September 10, 1970, a year to the day after we took over first place from the Cubs for the first time. This time, though, the other guys pulled away. The previous September we went 23–7 to roll past everybody. In 1970 we were 15–14 the last month and lost three straight one-run games in Pittsburgh in the final weekend.

After the Mets got over the hump of being lovable losers, there weren't any easy teams to beat up on in the division. Almost every team had someone, or several players, who could change a game on a dime. The Cubs had a terrific lineup. Even Montreal put together a decent team after that first season.

The Cardinals could hit. They were only a couple of years removed from back-to-back pennants. Somehow the Cardinals finished fourth in 1970 despite all that talent. At the top of the order was Lou Brock, and they'd acquired Joe Torre, who was a terrific hitter. Ted Simmons was just starting out when I was with the Mets, but he has to be one of the best switch-hitting catchers ever. On the mound Steve Carlton and Bob Gibson were stars; Mike Torrez and Jerry Reuss were just breaking into the major league rotation. Vic Davalillo, whom I knew from my Reds days, hit .311 off the bench for St. Louis. He was a great bat handler. And in 1970 the Cardinals added Richie Allen from the Phillies. He hit long home runs, and I still think he should be in the Hall of Fame. He's in that category of players I loved to watch take batting practice.

Pregame Show

On the road and at home, I always liked to watch players on other teams hit. The home team would have more batting practice time, so on the road I could actually watch a little more than when we played at home. I would watch batting practice all the time. Most of the good hitters then weren't just hitting to see how far they could hit the ball in batting practice. They understood that they could hit the ball out of the park without really trying to swing for the fences. What stood out with a guy like Hank Aaron was his concentration more than anything.

The problem we had at Shea Stadium watching guys take batting practice is that if there was a lefty batter, you couldn't really go on the third-base side of the cage because that was the visitors' side, and that was frowned up on. So you'd kind of move yourself around on the first-base side to get a good look at the left-handed batters at Shea. I'm sure I'm not much different than a lot of others guys who were watching those star opponents take batting practice. We didn't have extensive highlights from out-of-town games like they do now. We watched them bat in person, and we savored the chance.

One player I saw take a lot of batting practice when I was working for the Mets as a broadcaster was Dave Kingman. It was his second tour with the Mets in 1981. If he had cut down on strikeouts, he would have been incredible. He'd hit these monster shots in BP—and sometimes he'd hit them just as far in games. If he had just worked on hitting the ball to the opposite field, he still would have had a lot of home runs, but he'd have been a much better hitter. Kingman had a lot of ability. I wish he would have worked harder on his game. But you know, all of us can say that we'd have been better if we'd worked more on our game.

Pee Wee, Cleon, and Lumber

Back when I was in the minor leagues, Pee Wee Reese signed me to a contract to use bats from Hillerich & Bradsby, the makers of the Louisville Slugger. Pee Wee was from Louisville, Kentucky, and he was a natural to represent the company. I grew up watching Pee Wee, and it was a thrill to be talking to him as a kid in the minors—everyone knew him from all the World Series those Brooklyn Dodgers teams played in during the 1950s. He was known for his great glove at shortstop, but he had 2,100 hits and drew 1,200 walks on his way to the Hall of Fame. Which is to say, he also knew what he was talking about when it came to bats.

When I got to the Mets, I ended up using Adirondack bats much more than Louisville Sluggers. I started using them because Cleon Jones used them, and he talked me into it. He told it was a heavier bat, which would enable me to hit the ball to the opposite field. I started hitting the ball the other way with much more success than ever before. Teams used to put the shift on me, and it took me a while to realize there were a lot of hits to the opposite field. In 1969 I hit .300 for the only time in my career. The next year I batted .293 and had my best year in a slew of other categories.

Cleon was instrumental in a change that led to my two most productive years in baseball. He really knew his stuff. He was our left fielder, but he was probably the closest the Mets had to a batting coach in my time there—the team later hired him as a roving batting instructor in the minors. He worked on hitting with struggling minor leaguers such as Lenny Dykstra and Kevin Mitchell, who turned into solid hitters in the majors for years.

Thanks to Cleon's advice, I wound up having much more success with Adirondack bats than Louisville Sluggers. Baseball is a game of feel. No matter what someone tells you, you're going to use the bat that feels best in your hands. Both the Louisville Slugger and Adirondack bats were made of ash, but I thought the Adirondack wood was better. Or at least it felt better to me.

I ordered both Adirondack and Louisville Slugger bats. But I didn't have to drop the contract with Hillerich & Bradsby; I just ordered fewer bats from them. I always thought I'd get some blowback from Louisville, but no one ever said anything. Al Weis was also a Louisville Slugger guy, and he used a souvenir Adirondack bat during the 1969 World Series. He was told by Louisville Slugger to put pine tar up on the bat so you couldn't see the distinct circle on the Adirondack bat. Al wound up hitting a home run, drawing four walks, batting .455 against the Orioles, and winning the Babe Ruth Award. Maybe they should have gotten on me for using an Adirondack bat—or could it be that the pine tar made the difference for Al?

Driving Me Batty

My biggest issue with my bats wasn't who made them but who used them: pitchers!

All Mets pitchers took batting practice at Shea because there was extra time when we were at home. Pitchers didn't have bat contracts, so they used our bats. They broke bats all the time in BP. After a long home stand, I often had to reorder bats.

I sometimes hid my bats or took them home with me. If I had garage parking in the city, I'd leave them in the trunk of my car. Otherwise I'd take them with me to my apartment. If I parked on the street, I'd never leave the bats in the car—I'd rather let pitchers use them than have them get stolen!

Nodding to the Boss

When people ask me about our then-owner, Joan Payson, or then–chairman of the board, M. Donald Grant, I always say they were nice to me. I had very few conversations with them, though I saw them a lot around the ballpark or sitting in the stands near the dugout.

I always said hello to Mrs. Payson before games when she was there; it didn't extend much beyond "Hello, Mrs. Payson. How are you?" I have a wonderful picture of her, Tom Seaver, Johnny Murphy, and me at a function. I only saw her in the locker room once when we won the World Series—and she was only there briefly and retreated for fear that she'd get soaked by the champagne that was everywhere.

Mrs. Payson was always on the right side of the dugout, often sitting with Pearl Bailey, the singer. Pearl was a big fan of ours. You could see Mrs. Payson when you were warming up outside the dugout before the game. Whether she knew who I was or not is open to discussion. I remember seeing her a lot at the games.

The few times I had a conversation with M. Donald Grant, he was very friendly. I don't know if he knew who I was out of uniform, but I never had much interaction with him. Contract time was always with Johnny Murphy or Bob Scheffing.

Opening Supermarkets, Doling Out Trophies

When I played, few ballplayers made enough money not to have to hustle to make ends meet during the winter. We mostly did personal appearances, played on a traveling basketball team, and anything else that kept us busy and kept money coming in; $100 appearance fees back then were important.

The Mets sent people out into the community to attend Little League banquets, hand out trophies, pose for pictures, and handle speaking engagements that didn't tax our vocabularies or the audience's patience. Either the Mets paid us for going or the sponsoring organization paid us. It was not a lot, but it was steady—Long Island had a lot of recreation leagues. I can't begin to tell you how many Little League banquets I spoke at or what I said, but everyone was all smiles when you handed them a trophy. Eddie Kranepool and I did hundreds of things like that. If you lived in New York in the off-season, you were on the team's speed dial even before there was speed dial.

One day Ed Kranepool, Bud Harrelson, Ed Charles, Yogi Berra, and I appeared at a supermarket in New Jersey. Of course, Yogi was the big hit. We were outside signing autographs behind some tables, and the owner came over to us and asked, "You want me to fix you some sandwiches?" We all said yes. He got down to where Yogi was and said, "Hey, Yogi, what can I do for you?" Yogi said, "I want to take some stuff home—some meat." He brought Yogi a big shopping cart and told him, "Yogi, go take whatever you want."

The rest of us got cold cut sandwiches. We were all over Yogi about that. But Yogi was the king. It was Yogi's world, and the rest of us were just living in it.

In the years since, I became really good friends with Yogi's son, Larry, the oldest of his three boys. I am still involved in Yogi's golf event in New Jersey, which I try to play in every year. I did a recent personal appearance with Larry Berra in Florida along with Gil Jr. They were representing their dads, and I was there to add to what they said and to talk about the connection we all had with the Mets. I tried to help Gil Jr. and his family promote his father getting into the Hall of Fame, which finally happened—long awaited and much deserved.

Roommates

The assignment of roommates in professional baseball is . . . I don't know what the best word is to describe it. Cryptic? When kids go to college, they fill out questionnaires or the school has a whole elaborate system for determining the most compatible roommates. When I played, it seemed like roommate assignments were usually decided with a snap decision by a coach or traveling secretary. You might also find yourself rooming with a person whose name came right before—or right after—your name alphabetically. And sometimes you would just get asked who you'd like to room with.

And everyday players sometimes roomed with pitchers. In Cincinnati I was paired with Sammy Ellis. One year he won 20 games and the next season he lost 20 games. Well, I looked, and he actually lost 19 in 1966 after winning 22 the year before, but I'm sure we got him off the hook for at least one loss. I'd wake up in the middle of the night, and he'd be going through his curveball grip in the mirror. You couldn't turn on the air conditioner the night before he was pitching for fear it might do something to his arm.

I roomed with Ken Boswell during my whole time with the Mets; I don't remember how he was unlucky enough for that to occur. He was young and single, and I was a little older and married.

The worst thing Kenny and I did in terms of not following the rules was go somewhere we shouldn't—it could be a flight to Las Vegas during a West Coast trip, but more often it was just something to break the monotony of a road trip, such as going on the roof of the hotel to sit in the sun. We had to be very careful not to get sunburned. All you needed was to let Gil or one of the coaches see you were sunburned. A tan line on your arms was good—that meant you got your sun while wearing a uniform and doing drills, running laps, or playing in the field. But sunburn was a no-no; that was a dead giveaway that you'd spent too much time on the beach. Or on the roof.

Chapter 6

AN AMAZIN' RIDE

Topps

Topps was the only licensed product for baseball cards for many years, though dozens of card companies came along later.

During spring training in the 1960s and '70s, Sy Berger, a nice man who worked for Topps for more than 50 years, would come around and give you a booklet with some gifts for signing with Topps. Gifts weren't more than $250 or $300. You could pick out something like a portable radio or a 12-inch black-and-white TV; if the latter got one station, it was great.

It was a bad sign if the Topps rep skipped over your locker in spring training. A Topps rep would usually talk to some official with the club, who would give them an idea of who might be on the team for most of the year. If you weren't on that list and still made the team or stuck around the majors all year, then Topps might send someone to get shots of you later in the season. Or they'd use an old picture, which is what they did in 1967–68 when the players staged a boycott because of Topps's monopoly.

That boycott was one of Marvin Miller's first victories as head of the Major League Baseball Players Association. Players were signed by Topps in the low minors with a five-dollar binder that still applied if they were in the majors a few years later. Miller knew this was a problem, and he challenged Topps; they brushed Miller off, figuring he had no leverage. So for those seasons, the players wouldn't sign deals with Topps or pose for pictures. Topps wound up using the same baseball card pictures for multiple years because of that.

If you look at my Topps card from 1966, I'm in a posed batting stance in spring training. My 1967 card shows probably the next picture on the roll of film that the photographer took the previous year. My 1968 card is listed as "Mets"; it's me with my hat off, something Topps usually did during photo sessions in case you got traded—as I had just been after the 1967 season ended. My 1969 card shows a slightly different hatless picture—maybe taken during my first film shoot in 1965—cropped so you can't see the jersey logo, though it's clear I am still in a Reds uniform. Finally, in 1970, Topps used a posed photo of me swinging a bat as a Met—I know it was taken during the 1969 season because I have the 100th Anniversary of Professional Baseball patch on my left sleeve, which every team wore that year. That's the card I like most. It's a decent pose—as opposed to indecent, I guess.

My 1971 card is the only in-game card Topps ever printed of me. I'm trying to get out of the way of a pitch. Again, I don't know how they decided which picture to use. My last card—from 1972—says I was with the Cardinals, who'd traded for me the previous fall. You can see the underside of my cap and can't see my uniform logo, though any 10-year-old kid chewing the gum from the pack could tell you I'm in a Mets jersey. That's one of the few photo shoots I remember, because the photographer sat on the ground and seemed to aim at my Adam's apple while I stood over him.

The card I get asked to sign the most is my 1965 rookie card, which shows me with Dan Neville, a pitcher from the University of Kentucky who never reached the majors. Back then they put two prospects on one card and called them Rookie Stars. My second-most-popular card is not a Topps card at all—it's one I made myself: Mickey Mantle and me in uniform taken before the 1968 Mayor's Trophy Game. People who I show it to love it because it covers both teams from the game. It's a great calling card whether you're a Yankees fan or a Mets fan.

Have Glove, Will Travel

There was not much mystery or sleight of hand when it came to my dealings with Rawlings, the glove manufacturer; they were handled out of the back of a car. Since the Cardinals and the Mets shared spring training in St. Pete, the Rawlings rep could do both teams on the same day—he had to love that. The back of his rented station wagon was filled with gloves and shoes. You received two gloves and two pair of spikes. Just like with Topps, getting signed by Rawlings in my early days as a minor leaguer was how I figured out I was a prospect.

I knew Oscar Roettger as the white-haired Rawlings rep, but he'd played a few games with Babe Ruth on the Yankees and spent his final season with Connie Mack's Philadelphia Athletics. Roettger was born in 1900 and, like me, was from St. Louis. Players would be lined up in the parking lot waiting to see what he had in the back of his station wagon, and when I got up there he and I would talk for 20 minutes about growing up in St. Louis. Then he'd say, "Nice talking to you. Who's next?" He never gave me anything extra despite our St. Louis connection.

My first year, I got two outfield gloves. When I went to the Mets and Gil Hodges wanted me to play first base, I got one outfielder's glove and one first baseman's glove. That was fine, because I never needed more than one glove at either position in a year. I can remember I wore one glove with someone else's name on it: Jim Northrup, who played outfield for a long time for Detroit. Let it be noted that neither of us won a Gold Glove.

I guess it all had to do with how many gloves they were selling and whose name was on them. I'm sure that contract I signed let Rawlings manufacture a glove with my name on it if they thought it would sell. When you're 19 or 20 years old, who reads the fine print? We were at the mercy of trying to finagle a way to get some equipment.

Montreal, Hands Down

I had two operations on my left thumb from playing outdoors in cold weather. Growing up in St. Louis, there were no indoor facilities, so we'd play baseball in the cold and snow sometimes because we couldn't get enough of the game. I had a bad bruise on my left hand that turned into calcium deposits, and I had to have it operated on right after high school, during the short period I spent at the University of Missouri. I had another operation in 1962 in the minors and missed part of the season. So my hands were very tender. Because of the operations, I wore a batting glove on my left hand, though ballplayers didn't wear batting gloves too much in the 1960s. The cold could bother my hand if a pitch got in on my fists, but at the same time, that just gave me incentive to hit the ball on the good part of the bat.

With my hand issue, you'd think I would have hated going to Montreal and playing in Jarry Park Stadium, where you held your breath for those early- and late-season trips because the weather could certainly get bad for baseball. The park was tiny, and it got pretty frosty in April, but I loved Montreal. It was Canada; it was beautiful. Everything was good about Montreal, and you just accepted the ballpark.

Along with San Francisco—the city, not Candlestick Park—Montreal was my favorite place to visit after the Expos came into the league in 1969. The people in the stands were thrilled to have Major League Baseball. They had some good players. They were an expansion team, but they weren't like the Mets in '62—stuck with a lot of veterans at the end of the line; the Expos didn't make that mistake. They had some good players and seemed to have the best names in the league, such as Coco Laboy and John Boccabella. The announcers really did a great job with the names. The fans truly loved Rusty Staub, nicknamed Le Grande Orange. (It probably also helped my feelings about Montreal that I hit .297 there during my career.)

We stayed at the Queen Elizabeth Hotel when we were in Montreal. From there we could go right underground to the shopping center that seemed like it extended for miles. Or kilometers, I guess. Montreal knew how to deal with the cold and snow: move everything underground and pay the weather no mind. They had such great restaurants—aboveground and below. As for French-speaking Quebec, the people just looked at you and knew who was a French speaker and who only spoke English. Was it that obvious?

The Windlestick Error

I played three-quarters of my games in the outfield, and the rest were at first base. The Mets had Donn Clendenon and Ed

Kranepool to play first most of my time with the team, but Gil was the one manager I had who liked to put me at first base. In 1970 Ed Kranepool had a tough year and got sent to the minors during the season, and I played just about as many games at first base as I did in the outfield that year. Only Wes Parker of the Dodgers had a higher fielding percentage among major league first basemen than my .995, though I did not play as many games at first as many others. Committing only two errors for a guy who spent most of his career as an outfielder was an accomplishment. All those fungoes Gil Hodges rocketed at me paid off.

I remember my games in the infield so well because I got to interact with teammates instead of being on my own as I was in the outfield. But there were some moments when I wished I were playing under a rock—none more than on certain nights at Candlestick Park.

One night in San Francisco I was playing first base and the ball was popped up to the left side. It was one of those games when the wind blew in from left to right, but the ball started almost on the third-base line, and I assumed the third baseman or shortstop would catch it. Before I knew it, the ball had drifted over toward first. I wasn't ready for it, and the ball popped out of my glove. I'm still annoyed just thinking about it.

I dreaded that ballpark. I used to put cotton in my ears, and my eyes would tear sometimes when it was windy and cold, which was often. The Giants would play Tuesday and Friday night games. Those were horrible games to be part of. I believe Willie Mays would have had 800 home runs if he hadn't played most of his career at that ballpark. I told Willie something to that effect one day when I was holding him on at first base. He said, "You might be right, but I'm used to it."

The ballpark also didn't stop Willie McCovey, whom we called Stretch. The US Navy had a shipyard in the bay, way beyond the ballpark, where it repaired ships. Stretch was leading off first after ripping a single one time, and I asked him, "Are you trying to sink one of those boats out there beyond right field?" He just smiled. He wasn't much of a talker, but he was very much a respected slugger. Case in point: the part of San Francisco Bay beyond the right field wall at Oracle Park, where the Giants play now, was dubbed McCovey Cove, even though the team didn't move there until 2000, decades after McCovey had retired. The passage of time doesn't dim legends such as Stretch.

McCovey wasn't that tall, but he sure looked tall. He seemed to me like a towering figure—a larger-than-life person. He was listed as 6'4" and 198 pounds, but he looked more like he was 6'9" and 250. When he was playing first base, it was like the infield was tilted. He had a big presence.

The Giants had a great hitting lineup with McCovey, Mays, and Jim Ray Hart in the middle of the order. San Francisco also had Bobby Bonds, who quickly became a star. They had Jim Davenport too, and George Foster was just coming up, though they traded him to the Reds before his career got going. Their pitching staff was tough, with Juan Marichal and then Gaylord Perry the next day throwing that stuff he was throwing.

But Candlestick was a tough place to play, even as the home team. The day games were deceiving: They would start out beautiful; it'd be calm and 65 or 70 degrees in the middle of summer, whereas everywhere else we played during that time of year was 85 or 90 degrees, or even hotter. Then around 3:00 the wind would start to pick up, the fog would roll in, and suddenly we'd be at the mercy of the weather. And that carried over to the night games.

The city was beautiful—absolutely beautiful. The restaurants, the scenery, the people—everything about San Francisco was beautiful. Except for the ballpark. It was right out on the bay, completely exposed to the elements. I know the 49ers played football there for years, and the city even enclosed the stadium to accommodate the crowds and hoped it would make the wind less severe, but nothing short of a dome could make it more hospitable for baseball.

The Giants of that era put four guys in the Hall of Fame: Willie Mays, Willie McCovey, Juan Marichal, and Gaylord Perry—plus a fifth, Orlando Cepeda, who played there for eight years before he was traded to St. Louis in 1966. You'd have thought the team would have done better and drawn more people, but you had to have winter coats at those games at night, even in the summer. I never got used to it, and—no matter what he said—I'm not sure Willie Mays ever did either!

Dome, Abysmal Dome

The Astrodome looked pretty scary when you drove up to it on the bus from the hotel—like a flying saucer landed in the middle of Houston. It was hard to see when a pop-up was hit—and this was after they painted the roof, the grass died, and they invented a special artificial turf just for the place (what I would call extreme AstroTurf compared to the surfaces that came later).

The field in Houston was so hard that balls could bounce over your head if you came in too far. It was a big, big ballpark. It was not fun to play in. I hit one home run there, against Jack Billingham. It was such a tough place to see, let alone play.

The Astrodome was the first place I played where they had split doubleheaders. We'd have to sit around all day. One good thing was they had a guy in the clubhouse who put out food between games. There weren't many ballparks that did that.

At Shea we barely got anything between games of a doubleheader—I think we got soup. The breaks between games at Shea were about 30 minutes, and they didn't want us filling up, I guess. It was hard for us to maintain our energy on such little food while playing for six hours. It made me want to climb the railing and grab a hot dog from a vendor midway through the nightcap of a doubleheader.

And after the games at Shea, there was warm Rheingold on tap near the shower area. They switched to Schaefer kegs after they became our beer sponsor. I wasn't much of a beer drinker, so I didn't really care for it.

Mr. Clean Uniform: Bob Aspromonte

I have a trivia question: Who was the last Brooklyn Dodger to play in the major leagues? It's a tough one: Bob Aspromonte. He debuted in Brooklyn in 1956, and he was playing third base for the Mets in his final season in 1971. Bobby was from Brooklyn, and he had an older brother, Ken, who also played in the majors for a few years. Ken ended up as the manager in Cleveland. Bob wound up living in Houston and had a Coors distributorship—he did really well in his post-baseball career.

Bobby was a good-looking guy and should have been in the movies. What he was not was a get-your-uniform-dirty kind of ballplayer. We found that out one night when he was with the Astros.

The dugout at the Astrodome went from near home plate to all the way past third base. The dugouts were 120 feet long.

Supposedly, Astros owner Judge Roy Hofheinz wanted the dug-outs that long so they could charge more people more money for sitting right behind the dugout! I don't know about the fans, but the long dugouts gave the guys on the visitors' bench a close-up view of the goings-on at third base.

Bobby was Houston's third baseman for much of the 1960s. We discovered something about him on my first road trip with the Mets. It's hard to forget, because it was the first week of the 1968 season, and we had a never-ending 24-inning game at the Astrodome. We noticed that one inning, after Bob got dirty diving for a ball—in the 1960s the Astrodome infield was all dirt—he came back the next inning wearing a clean uniform!

Man, did we give him a hard time. The dugout was maybe 30 feet from third base. If you got on somebody, they could hear every word you said. We kept yelling at Bob that he needed to run back to the clubhouse to change. After a few innings of this—whether to make us happy or because he felt he had to—he did change his uniform. I miss that part of the game—the banter. They weren't confrontations; they were conversations.

I don't recall Bob getting his uniform dirty too often or changing it mid-game with the Mets in 1971. He was a really good teammate and was at the end of his career. He was at a point when he didn't slide so much or make a lot of diving plays anymore, so his uniform stayed pretty clean.

Though I admit I am still puzzled why Wayne Garrett didn't play most of the time at third base. Wayne was a good player. If they'd just let him play regularly, the Mets might not have felt they needed a third baseman so badly that they had to trade Amos Otis and then Nolan Ryan to find one.

Traded—Again

You always remember the first time you were traded, because you are being sent away from all you know about the game. You are as floored as if you heard someone died (except then you wouldn't have to move halfway across the country).

The second time you get traded, it is different. You already have the firsthand knowledge that professional baseball is indeed a business. And on a major league team, you will never be the only one who started his career with another organization. That's how teams are made—then and now.

You could assemble a 1969 Mets lineup from all the players acquired from other teams: Tommie Agee, Bobby Pfeil, Donn Clendenon, me, Ed Charles, Jerry Grote, Wayne Garrett, and Al Weis—with J. C. Martin coming off the bench. People remember our pitching staff for all the young pitchers we drafted and brought up through the minors, but we still had veterans acquired from other clubs: Don Cardwell and Cal Koonce, plus Ron Taylor—such a key piece to the team coming out of the bullpen to shut down the opposition late in the game. Lefty Jack DiLauro pitched a few big games for us in 1969, and he came from the Detroit Tigers.

Quite honestly, I don't remember how I found out the Mets had traded me to the Cardinals in the fall of 1971. I know Gil didn't call. But then, I didn't expect him to. That was GM Bob Scheffing's job, but I don't recall hearing from him either. I don't remember anybody calling me to tell me about the trade. The eight-player deal was orchestrated by Bing Devine. As Mets general manager he'd acquired me in autumn of '67—then left to become St. Louis GM.

The City for Me

I was going to my hometown ballclub: the St. Louis Cardinals. It was a kid's dream come true. Was I excited? No. New York was home now. October 16, 1969, the day we won the World Series, changed my life, and I was a New Yorker.

I can't speak for anyone else, but once I moved to New York City, it was city living for me. I didn't always feel that way. As a young player coming to play in New York with the Reds, the city seemed intimidating when we stayed in Midtown during road trips. Once I came to the Mets in 1968, the feeling was completely different. I fell in love with the city. New York became my home.

Not everyone I played with felt that way. Most of the other Mets lived in Queens. Tom Seaver lived in Connecticut. Most guys returned to where they grew up after the season. I couldn't imagine living anywhere other than Manhattan.

Even after the trade—the second trade, that is—I never thought about moving from New York. During the baseball season, players figured out where to live in the cities that owned our rights. Once the season ended, though, New York City was the place to be for me. My kids were going to school here. There was no debate about where we were going to live.

A Bad Fall for the Mets

I was not the only Met the team moved on from after the 1971 season. The Mets sold Ron Taylor to Montreal and released Bob Aspromonte and Donn Clendenon on the same day, plus during the summer of '71 the Mets had released Al Weis. But the big one that still may rank as the worst deal in team history was trading Nolan Ryan *and three other prospects* to the Angels for Jim Fregosi.

This deal had reverberations for years in New York, as Nolan, still only 24 at the time of the trade, instantly became one of the most feared pitchers in baseball. In the next three years, he fanned 1,079 batters in 122 appearances, winning 62 games (on a team whose offense wasn't any better than the Mets'), setting the all-time single-season mark for strikeouts in 1973, and throwing his first three no-hitters. And he was just getting started. He broke all kinds of records in a career that was as long as it was impressive, throwing his seventh and final no-hitter at the age of 44.

I think part of Nolan's success with the Angels was joining a different league, pitching regularly, and getting out of New York. I loved New York, but not everyone who lands in the city takes to it. I think Nolan was frustrated in New York. He was a down-home kid from Texas, and he got a chance to pitch in the American League. Though the AL had some good-hitting teams such as Baltimore, Detroit, and Oakland, I think the quality of the National League was very strong and harder to pitch against. A lot of greats—all-time greats—were still around in the National League in the mid-1970s. The National League was a tougher league. Nolan found success in the NL again when he was older.

After playing for the Angels through 1979, in 1980 he went to the Houston Astros, near his home, where he won two National League ERA titles in the 1980s. He had a great career—remarkable longevity while staying relatively healthy. That's the key. If you don't stay healthy, you can't do it.

He had really strong legs and lower body strength, which were the keys to his success. Just like Seaver. How many stud pitchers did the Mets produce in the 1960s? Ryan, Tom Seaver,

Jerry Koosman, and Tug McGraw—the average career for each of them was around 20 years!

Marvin Miller and the Strike of 1972

The baseball minimum salary in 1969 was $10,000. The average ballplayer salary was about $25,000. Ten years later, the minimum salary for a ballplayer had doubled and the average major league salary was up to $113,000. That progress is attributable to one man: Marvin Miller.

Miller had a long history with labor unions, including the United Steelworkers and United Auto Workers. He moved over to baseball and was elected executive director of the Major League Baseball Players Association. At the end of the 1971 season, he came around and talked to all the teams about the possibility of a strike in spring training. He was very soft-spoken, very low-key, and he talked to all of us, like it was a team meeting. What follows is not verbatim, but I'll always remember the general idea of this talk.

"There is a possibility that we might have to go out on strike," Miller said. "Baseball ownership has been set in their ways for so long, maybe that's the only way they can be moved. I know most of you are really worried about this. There's never been a strike before. But remember this: you are not only doing this for yourselves but for the players down the line—future players."

Nobody had ever been through anything like a strike before in sports. All of us were programmed into the one-year contract. We were with this team until they traded us or released us. They had all the control. It's totally different now.

There were only 16 major league teams when I signed in 1959. When I arrived in the major leagues in 1965, there were

20 teams. Then in 1969 they expanded to 24. Now there are 30 clubs, and there is talk about expanding more.

I played in the minor leagues in Triple-A baseball and had some really good years. I spent two years in San Diego, which was then Cincinnati's top minor league team. I'll never forget a conversation I had with Fred Hutchinson when he was managing the Reds and I was coming off a good season in Triple A. He said to me, "We really like you, but I've got to send you back to Triple A. Where are you going to play here? I've got Frank Robinson in right field, Vada Pinson in center, Tommy Harper in left, Pete Rose might play a little left field, and Deron Johnson may play out there too. Where are you going to play?"

So I wound up playing two years of Triple A baseball. But I got the chance to play against all these quality players who were in the same position because there was no room in the big leagues for them, either. The Portland Beavers, Cleveland's Triple A team in the Pacific Coast League, had a staff in 1964 of Luis Tiant (15–1, 2.04 ERA), Sam McDowell (8–0, 1.18 ERA), and Tommy John (6–6, 4.26 ERA); all of them struck out a batter per inning or better that year (except John, who just missed by two batters) and all of them would go on to memorable careers. And we beat them out by a game for the pennant in our division! Our lineup had Tony Perez, Tommy Helms, Cesar Tovar, and me. Every team had quality players, and we were all stuck there, waiting to make it to the big leagues.

So in spring training of 1972, the Major League Baseball Players Association took a big swing to try to change things. We stayed out long enough that the major leagues shortened the schedule. This was really the beginning of baseball allowing players to have all these opportunities: free agency, arbitration, the designated hitter—and all the new jobs that new spot in the lineup created in the American League.

We opened the doors. And I wonder how many people playing now even know the name Marvin Miller. Or appreciate what players did in 1972. That was the strike that led to free agency, and it really changed the game of baseball. Maybe 75 percent of baseball players today wouldn't know the name Marvin Miller. Wouldn't know it, wouldn't care.

Playing for the Cubs

You play against guys, and there's a perception they are the enemy. The rivalry between the Cubs and the Mets was really strong—especially in 1969, when they jumped out ahead of us in the first year of division play. We had these great games—Seaver against Fergie Jenkins, Koosman against Bill Hands—and the rivalry became so prominent. On top of that, we had a total dislike for their manager, Leo Durocher. I don't know specifically why we disliked him so much—maybe it was just because he was managing that team. Maybe part of it was because Gil and Leo had a history dating back to Brooklyn. Leo was an easy guy to dislike if you were on the other team. When I played in Cincinnati, we also hated the Cubs because of him.

And then I wound up playing for the team I'd loved to hate. The Mets traded me to the Cardinals, and then—as a result of the lockout between the owners and players—I was released by St. Louis at the end of spring training in 1972. The Cubs picked me up. I quickly realized that the players in the Chicago clubhouse were all good guys. They were just trying to win—same as we were on the Mets. I became friends with a lot of the players on that Cubs team. I still see Fergie Jenkins at his foundation's golf tournament, and the Mudcat Grant event in Binghamton, New York, which I go to every year.

A great character who was with the Cubs was Joe Pepitone. Joe was an All-Star and Gold Glove first baseman with the Yankees in the 1960s when I met him. Like me, his career was winding down with the Cubs in 1972. After Chicago he had a brief cup of coffee with the Braves before going to Japan to play for Tokyo's Yakult Atoms. I knew him both before and after he went to play in Japan, where he may have set back American-Japanese relations a few years with antics such as skipping games by saying he was injured, only to be spotted on the dance floor at a disco that same night.

Ernie Banks had just started as a coach when I got to Chicago in 1972. Ernie was a classic—he was old-school and a fun guy to be around. When I came to Wrigley as a visiting player, he was always saying, "There's sunshine and fresh air, so let's play two." One or another of us would always jokingly come back at him with, "If you play two today, you're going to lose two today." Ernie was just as jovial and good-natured in the home clubhouse as he was talking to you as an opponent on first base.

Ernie was a two-time National League MVP at short-stop, but he was exclusively a first baseman in the last half of his career; Don Kessinger took over shortstop in Chicago. It felt like if it wasn't Kessinger starting the All-Star Game and winning the Gold Glove, it was my Mets teammate Buddy Harrelson. And both could come through with hits at key spots. If you look up the 1970 All-Star Game box score, Kessinger and Harrelson each had two hits—no one else on the NL team had more than one hit in the game (which famously ended with Pete Rose scoring the winning run after his collision with Cleveland catcher Ray Fosse).

The Cubs had a great team: Banks at first, Glenn Beckert at second, Kessinger at short, Ron Santo at third, Randy Hundley behind the plate, Billy Williams in left, Jim Hickman in right. And when I was there, Billy North played a bit of center field as a rookie (he was traded to Oakland after the season and won a couple of world championships with the A's).

I believe Ken Rudolph was the backup catcher but don't remember him playing much for the Cubs. Hundley caught every day! He started 145 games a year as a catcher—and that was when you had doubleheaders almost every week.

The Cubs got tired. They only played day games at Wrigley Field. No lights. Blazing sun. Wind blowing out meant a potential slugfest. Wind blowing in could mean a pitchers' duel. Regardless of the conditions, Leo played the same lineup every day. The only exception was the starting pitcher—and Leo used a four-man rotation. The Mets, on the other hand, were the first to embrace the five-man rotation with Rube Walker and Gil Hodges. We may have been less experienced, but we were better-rested.

Tuned Out

Standing in the outfield at Wrigley Field in a Cubs uniform felt strange. I come across people all the time from Chicago. If we are talking about baseball, I ask if they are a fan of the Cubs or White Sox. If they are a Cubs fan, generally the person will say they know about the 1969 Mets and how we came from behind to grab the division title in the final weeks. They either witnessed it or have heard about it in agonizing detail. I tell them I played for the Cubs for a bit when Leo Durocher was the manager. It goes in one ear and out the other; they still want to talk about '69.

Before I even got to Wrigley in 1972, I'd played home games in a couple of the more difficult parks in baseball at the time. Of course, Shea Stadium had the airplanes flying over constantly. Those never bothered me, but I saw many visiting players let it distract them. They'd step out of the batter's box when an airplane flew over. As soon as that plane passed, another would fly over. You could stand there all day waiting to bat at Shea, but the umpires grew as tired of players stepping out as the fans did.

Crosley Field in Cincinnati, which stood until 1970, had an embankment in the outfield called the Terrace. It dated back to the 1910s, when people used to stand on the field when the Reds had overflow crowds. I learned right away that the best way to handle it was to have one foot on the terrace and one foot off. If you didn't do that, your knees would get closer to your body as you went back on the ball, and many an outfielder crumpled on the way up that incline. In such an instance, both outfielder and ball would land on the grass and base coaches would wave runners to take an extra base or two.

Crosley's unique feature was an early example in my career of having to be ready on every pitch. If you can eliminate distractions, you'll be a better player. I still tell kids that when I work with them at clinics.

In the outfield, you have to maintain concentration because you can go a whole game without a ball coming your way—and then suddenly there's a line drive tailing to your right with the game on the line. In Tom Seaver's 19-strikeout game in 1970, when he set a record by striking out 10 batters in a row to end the game, the only catch I had was the last ball the Padres hit in fair territory. It was a high fly by Cito Gaston in the sixth inning.

One reason I liked first base more than the outfield was because I got to touch the ball all the time. You don't need to tell yourself to concentrate, because there's a good chance that the next ball is coming to you. Gil Hodges hitting me those bullet fungoes at first base during infield practice ensured I was ready for anything hit in my direction.

So playing right field for the Cubs and having a moment during a pitching change, I contemplated about how different it was playing the same spot on the field with a big *C* on my chest as opposed to *New York* on my uniform. As soon as you got to the outfield as a visiting player, even just shagging balls in batting practice, the hollering started at top volume.

I remember being out there one sunny afternoon as a Met and hearing this gravelly female voice directly behind me, screaming:

"Shamsky, you suck!"

"You're gonna lose!"

"Cubs, Cubs, Cubs!"

It was so unrelenting that I eventually glanced behind me to say something back. I envisioned this horrible creature with these taunts, but it was a beautiful young girl in a bikini putting on suntan oil. She confirmed she was the one: "What are you looking at? The Mets suck!"

I was so stunned I didn't have the wherewithal to yell anything back; I just waved.

A Is for *Art*, *M* Is for *Mustache*

From Chicago I moved on to Oakland and started growing a mustache. A's owner Charlie Finley gave every player or coach a $300 bonus if they grew facial hair. They all grew mustaches and became known as the Mustache Gang. Although the offer was already over when I joined the team (it coincided with a promotion where every man with facial hair got into the Oakland Coliseum free on Father's Day that year), the A's gave me the bonus anyway when I grew my mustache. It was the first time I'd grown one. No ballplayers had grown facial hair in baseball in decades before the 1972 A's. The Reds had no one with a mustache for pretty much the entire 20th century, and the Yankees *still* have a rule against beards!

I wasn't in Oakland very long. The A's purchased my contract from the Cubs, and they used me as a pinch-hitter—the designated hitter wouldn't start in the American League until the following year.

The A's definitely had the most—and the most colorful—uniforms of any team I played for: three uniforms but no road grays. The A's only wore the home whites—white tops, white pants, and white shoes—on home Sundays. The other days of the week it was alternating green or yellow tops, both in Oakland and on the road. Manager Dick Williams and his coaches set themselves apart by wearing white caps with a green brim every day.

I'd been in the National League my whole career and hadn't played in American League parks. The first time I saw the Oakland Coliseum, I was wearing an A's uniform. On my first road trip with the A's, I saw Comiskey Park and Anaheim for the first time. I got to be on the other side of what I'd seen all those years from the Shea Stadium infield and outfield: a close-up view of a Nolan Ryan fastball. The one time I faced him, I popped up.

My one time up at Yankee Stadium, I walked to load the bases against Lindy McDaniel. Standing there at home plate, the fence looked so close in right field. It was a thrill for me playing at the old Yankee Stadium, and I would have loved to have spent time there. I had driven by it so many times over the years on the Major Deegan Expressway, but other than a Mayor's Trophy Game, I had never really spent much time on the field there.

I played a couple games at County Stadium in Milwaukee in 1965 when I was with the Reds; it was the year before the Braves moved to Atlanta. My first game back in Milwaukee was my last game in the majors, in 1972 (the Brewers were then in the American League). In the second game of a doubleheader on July 18, 1972, I pinch-hit against Jim Lonborg and grounded out to Brewers second baseman Bob Heise, who had played a few games with me as a Met in 1968 and '69.

The A's were as loaded with talent as they were with facial hair. Oakland had a lead of 8.5 games in the American League West. Dick Williams told me they were going to make a move, and I knew right then what it was: the A's released me the day after that at-bat in Milwaukee.

Whitey Lockman, who took over as manager of the Cubs after Leo Durocher was let go midseason, convinced me to go to Wichita, Chicago's Triple-A team, and stay in the game. I just wanted to see if I could still play. And I could, but I was miserable. I'd been all over the country, playing hurt, and missing the stability I'd had in New York. I didn't stay long. I was tired of baseball.

Billy Martin Has the Final Say

I didn't bat many times in Oakland. Manager Dick Williams only used me as a pinch-hitter—and I didn't get any hits. I wasn't doing well physically, and they had a great team (1972 was the first of three straight world championships for the A's). When I was released by Oakland, I called a couple people. One of them was Billy Martin. He was managing the Detroit Tigers, who would play the A's in the 1972 Championship Series. I called Billy at his team's hotel. He told me, basically, "Yeah, but you've been hurt. We can't take you on."

A friend of mine, who was with the Yankees in some capacity, mentioned my name to Elston Howard, who was a coach with the team. Ellie essentially told him the same thing Martin had told me: "Yeah, but he's got a bad back." That stigma was with me; I'd gotten that reputation of having been injured. Once you get that rep, it's hard to overcome.

Over the winter, I got much better, but I was so disillusioned with the game. After getting signed to play ball at 17, I'd been part of only two teams in my first 12 years: the Reds and the Mets. In my 13th year in pro ball, I was with three teams. It was not a happy situation for me. But in retrospect, I look back on it as a major regret that I didn't continue playing.

The medicine was not as good in the early 1970s as it is now—Tommy John was just a left-handed pitcher, not the name of a surgery that's been successfully performed on thousands of arms since then. Muscle pulls could sideline players for weeks. One-year contracts made many players reluctant to even talk about an injury, much less look for cutting-edge cures and take the time to heal properly. Team doctors weren't around all the time. And there was no track record that players came back as good or better after extended time being hurt. Many teams—such as the Tigers and Yankees—saw you as damaged goods once other teams had given up on you. The minor leagues were full of healthy bodies already on the rolls that could be summoned with a single phone call.

Looking Back: Regrets

I regret not working harder at the game. When I finished taking fly balls, I should have taken 10 more. When I was taking ground balls at first base, I should have taken 25 more. I regret not working more on my skills. Maybe I took things for granted. As I mentioned, one of my biggest regrets was not coming back to the game after the winter of 1972. I didn't try, and I should have. Adding years on my baseball pension should have been reason enough alone for coming back. Yes, I made a mistake, but I was lucky to play 13 years.

If this is a book about things I tell my friends, I'll say this again, because it is important: Work harder, and don't be satisfied. It all goes quickly. Baseball is your life. Make the next team, reach the next level, establish yourself, take care of your body, and earn enough for your family. Even though it was a struggle at times, it was wonderful. I should have come back.

But I have nothing to regret about how I live now—my life is good. Being part of that 1969 Mets team was so special. It was more than 50 years ago, and we're still talking about it. If I'd stuck around, maybe I could have come back to the Mets. Who knows? I didn't call the Mets again to see if there was any interest after '72. It didn't even dawn on me to call them. I guess I'd had enough, which was something, because I didn't have anything to fall back on outside the game. That's life.

Just like most people, there are things I wish I'd done differently. It seems obvious now. I was physically hurt when the Mets traded me to St. Louis. The 1972 strike hurt me, and I ended up with the Cubs and then Oakland. The whole season I was hurt.

That winter I didn't have an advisor or anybody to say to me, "You've got to go back. You're only 30." I ended up floundering and got into business ventures, many of which worked out. But they weren't playing in the major leagues. I didn't add years onto my pension. It made things tougher for my family and me.

I really screwed up. I didn't look at things clearly at the end of the 1972 season. I was so disillusioned with everything. Part of it was my fault that I wasn't close to anybody who'd tell me, "Hey, get out there. Work out. Work hard." The designated hitter was coming in, and salaries were starting to escalate. Arbitration and free agency were on the horizon. Just a couple years later, most players had agents. The situation for ballplayers was about to be better than it had ever been. I should have come back.

It hit me two or three years later that leaving when I did was a huge error, but by then it was too late. Like being the last out of a big game, you can't dwell on it. You move on, but you never forget. The game is so special when you're out in the field, looking at the crowd, feeling the sun on your face, concentrating on the pitcher, waiting to hit. A career seems to go by faster than a 3–2 pitch from Nolan Ryan.

Chapter 7

IN THE BOOTH: BROADCAST AND RESTAURANT

Broadcasting Starts with Seaver

Tom Seaver got me into broadcasting. Or maybe you could say M. Donald Grant got me into broadcasting. Grant was chairman of the board of the Mets and approved trading Seaver to the Reds on June 15, 1977. Right after the trade, Chet Simmons, president of NBC Sports, tracked me down and asked me if I'd like to work Seaver's first game with the Reds for *Game of the Week*. This was only a couple days away—Seaver had been traded at midnight Wednesday, and the game was Saturday afternoon in Montreal. At the time, I'd never done broadcasting or anything like it. I told Simmons, "Chet, I'm not sure I can do it."

"You'll be fine," Chet said. "We're sending you up there with Marv Albert. Marv will walk you through it. You played for both the Mets and the Reds, so you know the history, you know the players, you know the game. It'll be great." And Chet was right.

I knew Marv pretty well from my playing days, when he did the sports every night on WNBC-TV. That connection made me feel very comfortable. But I had no chance to practice, and I really didn't know what to do. Marv was wonderful and took control, making me feel comfortable right away. I'll say Tom certainly helped by pitching a three-hit shutout in just over two hours. The broadcast was so straightforward because there wasn't much to talk about. It was such an easy game to do, thanks to Tom. And Marv Albert.

That's when I got the broadcasting bug. I thought, *This is simple; I can do this.* It turned out it wasn't going to be so easy.

Mr. Laffs Himself

It was in 1969 that I first got involved in the restaurant business. One of my Mets teammates in 1968 was Phil Linz. He had played for the Yankees and the Mets—but he is forever remembered for playing the harmonica on the back of the Yankees team bus after a tough doubleheader loss in August 1964. Mickey Mantle told Linz that manager Yogi Berra's command was "Play it louder!" instead of the actual "Knock it off!" Yogi smacked the instrument out of Phil's hand.

Phil was a good player—baseball, not harmonica. He had to be good to emerge from the overstuffed Yankees farm system. After the harmonica incident, he took over at shortstop when Tony Kubek got hurt and helped lead the team rally from five games back to take the pennant. He was the leadoff hitter and shortstop in all seven games of the 1964 World Series, homering twice off Bob Gibson and Barney Schultz, respectively.

Well, by 1969 Phil was retired, and he had a place on First Avenue called Mr. Laffs. Phil made very good money. His original partners were no longer involved, and he asked me if I wanted to join him. I should add that this was after Phil and I had already opened a very popular club in New City, New York, called the Marshmallow, which we opened right after we won the World Series in '69.

We eventually ended up owning three places. The Marshmallow in Rockland County, Doubles in Queens, and Mr. Laffs in Manhattan. (I later opened another place downtown with Ron Darling in 1986, right around the time the Mets won the World Series that year. We named it after the address: 17 Murray Street. In retrospect, we probably should have called it Darling's.)

The Marshmallow was off exit 11 of the Palisades Parkway, about 20 miles from Shea. On the club's opening night, we had guest bartenders Tug McGraw and Wayne Garrett—Wayne was barely old enough to drink legally. The opening was incredible, with the elation of the '69 World Series victory still very fresh.

On Friday nights, Phil and I would make the rounds. We would go to the Marshmallow, then to Doubles, and then back into the city to Mr. Laffs. The Marshmallow had limited food, and Doubles and Mr. Laffs had full menus. It was great saying we owned three places, but in reality if we had concentrated on one place, we would have been better off. We sold the Marshmallow and Doubles, and I left Mr. Laffs in 1978, when I got more involved in broadcasting and I didn't have a lot of time.

When you own a restaurant, it's your business to go there all the time—every day, if possible. Phil understood. He left baseball because he wanted to concentrate on the restaurant business. After hitting .209 in 1968, he retired at not yet 30. Gil Hodges told him, "I want you to be on the team next year." But Phil decided he'd had enough. Like me in '72, he was very disillusioned with the game. I always used to say to him, "You should have played one more year and been on the '69 team." He agreed with me. He really would have reaped the benefits. Not so much financially as a player, but it would have been great for business.

Back in the mid-1960s and into the '70s, First Avenue on the Upper East Side of Manhattan was jumping. It was filled with nightspots such as T.G.I. Friday's (before it became a chain restaurant) and Maxwell's Plum. Mr. Laffs fit right in with so many places in a two- to three-block area.

Kenny Boswell was more a frequenter of nightspots than a restaurateur, but he certainly helped boost the profile of Mr. Laffs the night we won the World Series. Kenny went on TV with Sal Marchiano at WCBS after we clinched at Shea. Sal asked Ken, "What are you doing to celebrate?" Kenny said, "We're going to Mr. Laffs." They had to close down First Avenue at 64th Street because of the crowds.

No Agent as a Player; Now I Am One!

During my time in the restaurant business I was very sympathetic to actors working for me because in the 1970s I was in the talent agency business. It was called RLS after the initials for the last names of the partners: Cynthia Raglyn, Richard Landis, and me. Raglyn and Landis were working at a talent agency, and they happened to ask me to come in for a commercial. We became friends and then business partners, and I was in that business for a while. Landis left after a year or so, and we had a lot of top people sign with us for commercials, soap operas, and some movies. I started to get calls to do some work personally, especially in broadcasting.

It wasn't long after I got into the talent agency business that I realized that making 10 percent from actors was great if you had a big business, but it was not nearly as good as making 90 percent as an individual. I talked to Cynthia about this, and we both decided it was time for us to move on. She acted as my agent after I went to Channel 5. Unfortunately she passed away a few years later. She was really instrumental in my career transition into broadcasting.

Munson Announcement

I read the release about Yankees captain Thurman Munson's death on SportsChannel in August 1979, my first year with the cable network. I was handed a piece of paper and read it for the first time on the air. A plane crash. I didn't even know he was a pilot and had his own plane. My feeling was, *This can't be true. He was only 32 years old. He played last night!*

When you're young, it's hard to believe somebody who's younger than you can die. Now past my 80th birthday, it seems like every time the phone rings it's news that someone I know has passed away. It's hard to believe now, but it's harder to believe when you're young—especially when it comes without warning.

I knew Munson a little bit over the years. I remember he was catching in a spring training game with the Yankees in Fort Lauderdale. Fritz Peterson was pitching for the Yankees and hit me twice in the game. The second time he hit me, Thurman picked up the ball, looked at it, and said to me, "That couldn't have hurt, because I can catch him bare-handed."

A Close-Up View of the Rebuilding Mets

You'd think that working in the booth for the Mets would be a dream come true after the best days of my career were spent with that team, at that same ballpark. It was a tremendous opportunity, but during my broadcasting tenure, the Mets were not very good. They were accruing the draft picks in the minors that would blossom in the mid-1980s, but that didn't make it easier to watch and describe to the fans seeing the major league club struggle.

SportsChannel mostly broadcast the Mets during the week, and WOR-TV had the games on weekends. I sometimes worked games on weekends for WOR-TV. I started working for SportsChannel in 1979, a really tough year for the Mets. The period of 1979 to 1981 marked the beginning of cable TV leaping into the world of sports.

Unfortunately, the Mets lost 95-plus games during each of the first two years I was with SportsChannel; they lost the fewest in 1981, when almost 60 games were canceled by the strike. Even with the shortened schedule, the Mets still had a winning percentage under .400. Yet the Mets actually competed in August and September due to the split season—throwing out the results when the strike hit in mid-June and starting over in the second half in August. Many lower minor leagues historically started over in midseason, but this had never happened in the majors. I'd venture to say—or at least I hope—it won't happen again.

During those early years of cable in New York, there was not a big audience—it was new, not many people had cable, and many parts of the city wouldn't even be able to get cable TV for several years. But we helped draw people to cable, and the audience grew a little at a time—kind of like those early 1980s Mets teams, which improved very, very slowly.

When I started in 1979, I worked with Bob Goldsholl, who was also the sports information director at New York University. He had led NYU to the College World Series as a pitcher in the 1950s. In the winter of 1980, Nelson Doubleday

Jr. bought the Mets and Fred Wilpon came in as club president. I was there for the regime change, and though many things stayed the same, one change was getting to do games with Steve Albert. He was a really good guy, and we did a lot of traveling together covering the Mets.

The Mets were so bad that it was hard to get people into the game. Back then, like now, New York baseball fans were smart; you couldn't fool them into thinking the team was good. I always tell people that a good broadcast is when your team wins. When your team loses, the broadcast is only so-so. The silver lining was the people I worked with. I am forever grateful for the chance to learn from the best: Ralph Kiner and Bob Murphy, two legends, as well as true gentlemen, who were so helpful to me.

In the Booth

I worked with Ralph Kiner and Bob Murphy in 1980 and '81. They were still doing both television and radio. In the next couple of years, it shifted so that Ralph only did TV and Bob handled the radio every game.

They were both great to work with. And of course, they had broadcast Mets games when I was on the field. Ralph was a real hero of mine when I was growing up watching him play for the Pirates. I do recall one game Ralph and I were working when the Mets were taking on the Cubs at Shea, and we went to a commercial. When you come back from a commercial, you usually set the scene and say the inning and the score—that kind of thing. When the commercial was over and the director said we were back, Ralph said, "Here we are at Forbes Field with the Pirates taking on the Reds." He got the team and the stadium wrong! I didn't say a word. Ralph was in the Hall of Fame—I wasn't going to correct him; that was legendary director Bill Webb's job. Webb yelled into the earpiece, "No, Ralph! It's Shea! It's the Mets!" Ralph simply restated it and just kept on going. He was a pro.

By that point, Ralph had been in the Mets booth for 20 years. He'd seen those dreadful teams in the early 1960s, and then after a few great years (which I had been lucky enough to be a part of on the field), the team went back in the tank in the late 1970s. By 1980 or so, the team was awful, with new ownership coming to grips with what they'd bought and the franchise in the middle of the endless process of starting from scratch. Like I said, if it's a bad team you're working for, you can't fool anybody; it's tough to make a good broadcast. But if you talk to Mets fans who stuck it out through those years—or any of the 50-plus years Ralph broadcast for the team—they all still think of him like an uncle who taught generations of kids about baseball. It was amazing to listen to him tell stories about some of the greatest players and personalities ever—for example, Honus Wagner was his coach, Al López was a team-mate, Hank Greenberg was his mentor, Branch Rickey was his boss, George Weiss hired him to broadcast the Mets, and Casey Stengel kept him laughing. Lots of Hall of Famers. He brought them to life for people sitting at home; he taught them about the greats, whether they'd played in the 19th century or just passed through town the day before.

I had so much respect for Ralph as a player, as a broadcaster, and as a storyteller. I grew up a big fan of his in St. Louis when he was starring for the Pirates as the National League's biggest slugger. He hit all those home runs, and he just seemed so smooth with everything he did. And he was a Hollywood legend. He dated a lot of starlets, he lived in Los Angeles, he was young, he was good-looking, he had his winters free, and he hit a *lot* of home runs. That was quite a combination!

Imagine how big a star he would have been if he weren't stuck with a dead-end team in Pittsburgh and didn't have back problems. I can relate to back issues slowing down your career. Ralph still managed to put up incredible numbers—he already had almost 300 home runs before he was 30. And that included him missing almost three years as a navy pilot. No one ever has—and probably no one ever will—match his record of seven straight league home run crowns. He did it his first seven years in the major leagues—after he got out of the service in World War II! He was one of a kind. He was a pretty rare breed for any era.

I watched him hit all those home runs, play in the All-Star Game every year, and then when I got to the major leagues, there he was interviewing me in his own studio in the ballpark. And he was paying me to do it! For appearing on *Kiner's Korner*, you would receive certificates for gasoline or milk—yes, milk (Dairylea was a sponsor). It wasn't very extravagant, but when you're not making a lot of money, anything free is good. Those were things the family could use. But none of that really mattered—talking baseball with Ralph on the air was the real prize. And I was so fortunate to get to do it so many times as a broadcaster after my playing days were over.

How About That?

During the baseball strike in 1981, while I was broadcasting Mets games, SportsChannel needed programming, so they sent me to Tokyo twice in 10 days to call Japanese league games. The first time I flew to Japan was with Mel Allen, the legendary Yankees broadcaster and the longtime host of *This Week in*

Baseball, a nationally syndicated highlights show that predated ESPN, back when you rarely saw highlights from teams outside your own market. We didn't broadcast live but taped the games, and somehow they made their way back to Cablevision.

Fourteen hours on a plane is a long time, but I have to say the first trip over was interesting—Mel made it interesting. He had so many stories from his decades broadcasting the Yankees and being part of the game. But at some point during the flight there, I fell asleep, and when I woke up he was still talking. He didn't even know I was out. He was used to working a one-man booth.

And then 10 days later I went back to Japan, but this time it was with Steve Albert—Marv's younger brother. I got a chance to meet Sadaharu Oh, who was managing the Tokyo Giants. That was a big thrill for me—he hit 868 home runs and was revered in Japan. We taped those games and sent them back over to the US. From there they sent me to Norfolk to cover Tidewater because the minor leagues were still playing despite the strike. They were willing to cover whatever other sports they could find to put on the air. It was challenging to constantly cover different leagues, but it was the same game whether it was in Japan or Virginia.

A Frank Meeting

As soon as that last Mets game of 1981 was over, someone came to me and said, "Frank Cashen wants to see you." I really didn't know him—Frank had been hired as general manager in 1980. He hadn't hired me to broadcast Mets games, but I had probably met him at some occasion such as the Welcome Home Dinner. When I went into his office, he didn't belabor the point—he let me go, along with Steve Albert. The Mets certainly weren't going to fire Ralph Kiner or Bob Murphy.

I could see the frustration in Ralph during those seasons I'd broadcast with him. Like Murphy, he'd been working Mets games for almost 20 years by that time, and the team had gone from laughingstock to world champion to steady contender and back to laughingstock. Better days were coming for Ralph, Bob, and the Mets, but I wouldn't see them from the booth.

That last day of the 1981 season, Cashen also fired Joe Torre, manager of the team since 1977, and his coaches— including Rube Walker and Joe Pignatano, who'd been with the Mets since 1968. The Mets also fired Bob Gibson, who worked with Rube—Torre had called Gibson the team's "attitude coach." Getting fired is never pleasant, but to be fired on the same day as Hall of Famers Gibson and Torre, plus legendary coaches Rube and Piggy, was no disgrace.

Those coaches followed Torre to the Braves, who'd fired their manager, Bobby Cox. The following year Atlanta won a division title for the first time since 1969.

Sports Extra

I worked at Channel 5 for about nine years, until the station, Metromedia WNEW-TV, was taken over by Fox in 1986. *Sports Extra* was my longest recurring gig in the media world. The show aired every Sunday for decades—a version of it still airs at the same 10:30 PM weekly time slot. *Sports Extra* is a weekly roundup of the world of sports and predated all the sports programs that are on the air now—before ESPN or even SportsChannel.

I'm still so thankful to the producer, Norman Ross, who gave me the opportunity to work on *Sports Extra*. The show was a chance to cover everything from the World Series to the Super Bowl to the U.S. Open tennis championships—men, women, kids, even horses. I got to cover all kinds of different sports, including the pre-Olympics trials in Lake Placid in 1980, the Super Bowl, women's golf, men's golf championships, and basketball—I covered St. John's, Georgetown, and Villanova when the Big East had three teams in the Final Four and Villanova pulled off the epic upset in 1985. I interviewed a lot of the top professional and amateur athletes because of *Sports Extra*. I remember interviewing Tracy Austin when she was 14, her first time making the U.S. Open quarterfinals. She is still the youngest player to win a singles championship in tennis; at 16 she beat Martina Navratilova in the 1979 semifinals and Chris Evert, who had won the last four Opens, in the finals. That was a great story, and one of so many I was lucky to cover.

The Yankees' postseason success kept me busy. And in my last couple of years at Channel 5, it was great to see firsthand as the Mets became a power again after the down years.

I covered the Islanders a lot during those four years in a row they won the Stanley Cup to start the 1980s. I was a big hockey fan and really enjoyed reporting on the Islanders—even though I was a Rangers fan. I got to know all those guys on the Islanders: Clark Gillies, Mike Bossy, Billy Smith, Bob Bourne. Plus Gillies and Bourne had both played minor league in the Astros organization, so we had a little camaraderie talking about baseball in the locker room.

Those were fun times for me. I got my feet wet in broadcasting and really enjoyed doing features for Sunday nights and specials.

Pinch-Hitting on the Air

I am sitting on the bench during a game, and out of the corner of my eye I see Gil Hodges look at me and indicate I would be up next as a pinch-hitter and he is counting on me to come through cold off the bench. Being called by a TV network to fill in for someone was not nearly as nerve-racking. It happened several times over the years—that's how I first got involved in broadcasting—and usually I had a lot longer than a minute to get ready.

I'm always around New York, so I was called in to pinch-hit for several different broadcasting outlets over the years. In the early 1980s, when ESPN was just starting out, I was brought in to do some in-studio World Series commentating. I can't even tell you which World Series it was, but I remember going to their headquarters in Bristol, Connecticut. The preparation, the studios, the budgets—it was nothing like now. I was in the cable TV game when the sets looked like they'd been put together in someone's basement.

Then decades later, WPIX called me in one day for their weekend coverage of the Mets. I interviewed Zack Wheeler when he was a prospect. During the interview, he was admiring my 1969 World Series ring. I said to him, "You want to try it on and see how it fits? You may end up with one of these one day." He's come close.

What's interesting is the Mets had so many big, strapping young pitchers—Jacob deGrom, Noah Syndergaard, Matt Harvey, and others—that Zack almost became an afterthought. He was hurt when the Mets went to the 2015 World Series, but he has since pitched in a World Series for the Phillies, although they lost. He recently signed a three-year contract extension for $126 million in Philadelphia. Remember when I wrote about Marvin Miller speaking to teams about a possible strike in spring training in 1972 and how he said if it were to happen, it would be not only for us but for players down the line? Marvin really knew his stuff! When I was playing, *all of MLB* was barely worth $126 million.

An Original Voice of WFAN

I was there the day WFAN, the country's first all-sports talk radio station, went on the air on July 1, 1987. Before that day, 1050 had been country music station WHN, which carried Mets games. WFAN's tenure at 1050 was short-lived, and the all-sports station moved down the dial to 660 in 1988.

I hosted the early afternoon hours in the very early days of WFAN at my restaurant, 17 Murray Street. It was difficult for me because I was running the restaurant and trying to do the show at our busiest time of the day. It was so noisy that we only ended up doing it for a little while. I had to make a decision, and I moved on.

During my time on WFAN, booking guests for the show was pretty easy because they would come to my restaurant to do the show, and their gift for appearing was a free meal. We had some good guests. I took some calls at the restaurant too. The station's production was in the beginning stages, and sometimes it was good and sometimes it wasn't so good. The station told me they had to take my show out of the restaurant, so I was only on the station for a couple of months. I'm proud I was part of a pioneering concept that really took off, to put it mildly.

Original WFAN Lineup, 1987

Morning Drive	Greg Gumbel
10:00 AM to 1:00 PM	Jim Lampley/Spencer Ross
1:00 PM to 3:00 PM	Art Shamsky
Afternoon Drive	Jim Lampley/Pete Franklin
7:00 PM to 12:00 AM	Howie Rose/Mets Baseball
12:00 AM to 6:00 AM	Steve Somers

The initial concept of sports talk radio made some people nervous, thinking it wasn't going to work. Not everybody was on board. The *New York Times* did not give WFAN a rave review in its first week on the air, writing, "Those who tune to 1050 on the AM dial get mostly opinions of callers and hosts, a sometimes painful, repetitive exchange interrupted only by commercials and, every 15 minutes, the latest in sports news. Met games, which the station continues to broadcast, are the only long break from the chatter. Do we need this?"

Time has told us that we did, and we do, need this. Most everybody on the list of original hosts went on to bigger and better things. Sports talk radio and WFAN has turned into a gigantic product now. In addition to still being at 660 on the AM dial, The FAN, as it is known, is even on FM at 101.9.

In the beginning, Peter Beilan, a TV agent, called me about going on WFAN. I knew Peter, and he knew the people who were starting up the station, and I decided to do it with them. I was already working on Channel 5 on *Sports Extra*, so why not radio? I thought it would be a good opportunity, but as I said before, it was too much to manage with my restaurant too.

So I got in and out of the radio business, and eventually I got out of the restaurant business too. Everything in life is timing. The timing was right for me being a Met in 1969. Whenever I think I wasn't lucky about something, I just think about how fortunate I was to be in Flushing when lightning struck and the world saw it happen. That's something that's never far from my mind.

Ball Four

Jim Brosnan was the first player to write inside stories. He was in Cincinnati while I was in the Reds minor league system, but our paths didn't really cross. He wrote three books, of which the best-known is *The Long Season*.

Though Brosnan started the trend of writing about the real baseball dirt, former Yankees pitcher Jim Bouton's *Ball Four* was the first baseball exposé on the locker room, and it was much more detailed than Brosnan's books were. When WFAN went on the air in the mid-1980s, Jim Bouton was on the afternoon show with me a few times. The station was experimenting with Jim, and he came down from Massachusetts so we could do a few shows together. I enjoyed Jim. He was a character, and a little off the wall.

Bouton's was the first book that really showed the vulnerability of ballplayers, particularly Mickey Mantle. As kids we all idolized the players, never thinking that they had lives other than simply being these great ballplayers we wanted to watch. Jim's book really opened the door on all these other things that went into life in the locker room and players' personal lives. I don't know if that turned out to be a good thing or a bad thing.

From my point of view, if guys were great ballplayers, then I only really wanted to know about them as ballplayers. I wasn't concerned about their personal lives. I relate it to movie stars: When I'd go to the movies, the stars were bigger than life. Then I'd see them on *The Tonight Show Starring Johnny Carson* getting interviewed by Carson. I'd think to myself, *I don't care about this*. I just wanted them to be the stars. I think that happened to sports: personality surpassed performance in the public eye.

Rusty's Frog Legs

Rusty Staub and I became very good friends after we got out of the game. He was a terrific hitter—a great player. Rusty was very charity-oriented. I used to play in his golf event all the time. He did so much for Catholic Charities and the Catholic Church. His work with the New York Police and Fire Widows' and Children's Benefit Fund was already going before 9/11 and helped raise millions after the tragedy.

We ate a lot of meals together, and I can say that, without a doubt, he was the fastest eater I have ever met in my life. Whenever we went out to dinner, he would be done with his meal by the time I was two bites into mine. He was forever contemplating more food. Rusty was always goading me to try something new. I'm pretty basic—at least when it comes to food.

One time we went out to a nice place to eat, and he said, "I'm going to get some frog legs, and I want you to try some." I grumbled, and he replied with the line people always give when they want you to eat something that you want no part of: "It tastes like chicken."

He ordered the frog legs. When they arrived—two on the plate—I looked at them and then at Rusty. "There's no way I'm going to eat that," I told him.

Before the words were even out of my mouth, he was done with his and was looking at mine.

Met at a Restaurant

I always liked the challenge of running a restaurant. It's really a service business. You have to make sure the food is good and the service is good. It's your baby. The thing about the restaurant business that people don't understand is that when you get there in the morning and prepare to open, you have to hope your chef shows up, your bartender shows up, all your restaurant workers show up, your refrigeration is working, and all your machines are working. People walk into a restaurant to sit down and eat, and unless they have been in the business, they have no idea how difficult it can be just to open. Especially when you open for lunch, because there isn't a lot of time before people start arriving and calling.

I learned how to be a short-order cook, a bit of a plumber, not much of an electrician, and at times a busboy. You can have a bad location and even mediocre food, but the one thing you cannot have is bad service. You have to make the people working for you understand that. It's not only a reflection on them but on the owner as well. Good service can sometimes override things that go wrong.

Red and Foley's

Red Foley was a terrific writer for the *Daily News*. He was a really nice guy and the longtime official scorer for the Mets while working 10 World Series. I always had a good relationship with him and never had an issue with him scoring an error on me in the field that I didn't deserve or an error charged on a ball I hit that I thought should have been scored a base hit. I remember he used to comment to me around the batting cage before games that he thought I was a really good hitter. He was impartial because he was a writer—and the scorer—but he always said nice things to me when I saw him, which I appreciated.

Being a scorer is a thankless job in many ways, but he was good at it. There was a nice restaurant near the Empire State Building that was named Foley's after Red. They said it was "an Irish pub with a baseball attitude." Shaun Clancy ran it. Foley's was like Mantle's in Midtown. Both had nice runs in New York, but the restaurant business is tough. You have to love it and work at it—if Red were still around, he'd probably say that being an official scorer was a lot like that.

A Darling Establishment

While he was pitching for the Mets, Ron Darling was part of a group with me that owned 17 Murray Street, as I wrote earlier. The restaurant was downtown in Manhattan between Broadway and Church, near City Hall. The place was quiet at night and was closed on weekends because downtown was quiet then; now that area is very popular. The restaurant had a full menu and did really good lunches. We had a room downstairs for parties, and that saved us. We did a lot of closed-circuit-televised fights in that room downstairs; those were great nights.

I met Ronnie through mutual friend Tony Ferrara, who threw batting practice for the Mets and the Yankees. I would run into Ron through various events, and we became very good friends. I talked to him the night before he started Game 7 of the 1986 World Series against the Red Sox. I felt I could provide encouragement after living through that myself with a Mets team that was the toast of the town.

Even though I had been out of the restaurant business for a while, I decided to try it again right after the Mets won the World Series in '86. The 17 Murray Street ownership group comprised Ron Darling, Tony Ferrara, me, and Jerry Casale, a former pitcher for the Red Sox. Ron was known as Mr. P, or Mr. Perfect, by his teammates because of the way he carried himself: first-round draft pick out of Yale, the cover of *GQ*, well-dressed, and always eloquent. In baseball there are a lot worse nicknames. Lou Gehrig was one of the all-time greats, but while the press called him the Iron Horse, his teammates called him Biscuit Pants. Ask 1940s pitcher Johnny "Ugly" Dickshot if he'd swap nicknames with Mr. P.

I always had a pretty close-knit relationship with Ron. I'm really happy he had so much success on the field and in the booth. His brother, Ryan, worked for us as a bartender at 17 Murray Street while he was at college. Ron left the restaurant business after a couple of years, as did Jerry Casale. Tony and I continued operating the place, and we finally sold it 1992. That was the last restaurant I owned.

Ed Charles's Drink of Choice: The Glider

Before we sold 17 Murray Street, we renamed it Legends. I still have a menu from that time, when Tony Ferrara and I were running the place after Ronnie Darling and Jerry Casale had left. Overall, we were open from 1986 to 1992. Beer was $3.25, wine cost a quarter more, and the most expensive thing in the place was Dom Perignon for $100 a bottle. We had three specialty drinks that were named for individuals: Pele's Ultimate Margarita, Henri "the Rocket" Richard's Strawberry Excitement ("strawberries and rum like you you've never had them"), and the Glider. The Glider was basically a Long Island Iced Tea: vodka, rum, gin, tequila, and triple sec. The menu called it "the smoothest thing NY City's seen since Ed 'the Glider' Charles played third base for the Mets."

The Glider was served in a special glass the drinker could keep. The drink was so popular that we were constantly running out of glasses. The drink cost $4.50. Now it would be a $16 drink, and without the glass! In New York, at least.

Ed Charles was so proud of that Glider. He would come to the restaurant with an entourage of people. He truly was a wonderful and inspirational person. He spent a lot of years in the minor leagues just to get to the majors. Ed was a solid third baseman, and he might have been a star too, if the Milwaukee

Braves, who signed him, had brought him to the majors when he was 20 instead of 29. Who knows how good he would have been? He hit .291 in nine seasons in the minors, bouncing around for teams in Texas, Florida, Kentucky, hearing God knows what racist remarks from the stands—even at his home parks—and so many other indignities. After three years at Triple-A, one of the worst teams in baseball—the Kansas City A's—convinced the Braves to trade him. Ed finally debuted at 29 in 1962 and batted .288 with 17 home runs, and the A's won 11 more games than they had in 1961.

I saw what happened to Black and dark-skinned Latin players in the minors with Macon (Georgia) in the South Atlantic (Sally) League. We had to take them to different hotels, different restaurants, different bathrooms. I look back at that period of my life and I say, "Why didn't you stand up for your friends and teammates in that position? Why weren't you more forceful?" I don't have an answer, except that we were all so young and just trying to get to the next level. We were all so preoccupied with our own lives.

Our team in Macon traveled in station wagons between other Southern cities. Basically, we were just playing ball and doing what we loved to do, but it was a dark period for people who saw it firsthand.

That's why Ed Charles's humility was so great. He was the guy in the Mets locker room who would put his arm around you and comfort you when you were having a bad day. That was one of the wonderful things about him—besides being a terrific ballplayer. I loved Ed Charles because of who he was and how he acted and how he was the calming force in the raucous clubhouse that was one of the youngest in baseball. The average age on the 1969 Mets was 26; Ed was 10 years older—not to mention far wiser than any of us.

His even-keel personality was phenomenal. I was surprised he didn't continue to play more after 1969. I don't know if it was because the Mets didn't want to have him there or didn't think he could still play, or if it was him saying he didn't want to play anymore—I can't imagine that being the case. He was only 36. He made some great defensive plays in the World Series. He started four games against the Orioles. He only had two hits, but they were both in Game 2. He started the winning rally with two outs in the eighth inning of Game 2—the game we *had* to have. After scoring the go-ahead run on Al Weis's hit in the top of the ninth, he made a nice play on a tough short-hop ball and threw out Brooks Robinson for the last out.

You know what I remember about him at third base? No matter who was running from home to first—it could have been the slowest or the fastest guy—Ed always got him at first by half a step. I don't know how he did that. He just had that lob over to first, and he knew he was going to get the guy.

Tug McGraw really brought this out—it was like he was Ed's advance man. Tug would scream across rooms, on planes, on buses, wherever we were. Things would be relatively quiet, and then all of a sudden Tug would scream out, "Don't ever, don't you think about it, don't ever, ever, ever, throw a slider to the Gilder!" Even years later when we got together at events, you could be anywhere and Tug would do it—and do it dramatically (as with the poem "Casey at the Bat," which Tug performed a few times later in life).

I don't know how much Ed liked it, but Tug would always remind anyone within hearing distance that Ed Charles was important. The Glider would just sit there and smile, saying, "Aw, Tug." When I used to do it to him, he'd say, "Artie, come on!"

The Glider nickname actually came from Koosman. He must have been a rookie, while Ed was the oldest player on the team. In one game after he made a nice play, Koo said to him, "You know, you always seem to glide after the ball. That's it! You're the Glider!"

I had nothing but admiration for Ed on the Mets, and I'm sure everyone on the team felt something similar. Because he could have been bitter about what he had to go through and how much time he lost proving himself over and over—but Ed Charles was anything but bitter.

Ed and Donn Clendenon were roommates on the road in 1969. It was a great pairing. Clendenon was the instigator; the Glider was the pacifier. Donn stirred the pot; Ed turned down the fire. However you want to put it, we couldn't have done what we did without the two of them on that team.

I always thought Ed would have been a great conduit in the commissioner's office in something such as community relations. He served as a scout for the Mets and was a coach in the low minors. His main work was working with children in the New York City Department of Juvenile Justice and with Youth Options Unlimited in the Bronx. He was perfect for that. But there were 50 jobs for which he would have been perfect.

Ed was also known as the poet laureate of the Mets. I don't recall a lot of his poetry when he on the team—other than his poetry in motion, gliding over to cut off a ball in the hole—but I came across this, which can apply to everyone who has ever played the game:

An Athlete's Prayer
by Ed Charles
So guide me dear author for the competition is keen,
And I too might fall like others I've seen.
For many are the performers, yet few reach the top.
But with you leading the way, I cannot be stopped.
Amen

Chapter 8

THE 25TH ANNIVERSARY CELEBRATION SAGA

A Miraculous Idea Is Born

The first significant baseball card show I recall doing was for Gloria Rothstein at Chelsea Piers for the 20th anniversary of the 1969 team. It was held at Pier 92 on March 17, 18, and 19, 1989. It had not been even three years since the Mets won the 1986 World Series. The club had been to the NLCS the previous fall, and Shea Stadium was the first ballpark in New York to draw three million fans in a season. The Mets were hot. Combine that with nostalgia for the first Mets championship, and the lines of people waiting to see us went on forever.

That card show was the catalyst for me to understand how important and popular the 1969 Mets are to the history of baseball. We teammates from that 1969 squad had a great time seeing each other—as is always the case when we get back together—but the real takeaway was the reaction from the fans. It was as if 1969 had just happened. I hadn't seen Mets fans lined up like that since the last time I played in a Banner Day doubleheader!

I saw the adulation and admiration from the throngs of people wanting to talk to us and get various signed things by us 20 years after the '69 Series. I saw how significant this team is to baseball history, and that was the beginning of me wanting to write the book *The Magnificent Seasons*, about the world championships by the Jets, Mets, and Knicks between 1969 and 1970. I really enjoyed writing that, and though it was not published until 2004, the idea for it was planted at Chelsea Piers in 1989.

The people who come to card shows are some of the same people who come to my book signings. I appreciate the support and the idea that something I did or was a part of 50-plus years ago is still felt by people. These connections come one after the other as the fans make their way up to me to sign. It's a combination of collectors who think signatures are worth money now and will be in the future, plus those fans simply taken with adulation for me and the team I played on. I have signed every piece of baseball memorabilia you can think of, and some people want money signed for whatever reason. I have even signed a body part or two—that's as much as I'll say about that.

I think the 1969 Mets are one of the few teams that can come together decades later and still have lines of people wanting to talk to them. Most of the people who attended the 1989 card show at Chelsea Piers were around when we won. To them—and to us—years later, this team still symbolized something special.

Met at Mantle's

Fast-forward to Mickey Mantle's Restaurant in early 1993. I met Ed Schauder, a bright, young attorney who had graduated from Columbia University, at an event at Mantle's on Central Park South in Manhattan. Mantle's was always a place for special events. Over the years I had gone there for simple meetings as well as for many charity and press events. I don't recall what this one was about, but in any case, that is where the Shamsky/Schauder connection started.

Ed had grown up a Mets fan and had already tapped into the world of sports with his efforts in 1990 to recognize and celebrate the Negro Leagues and former Negro Leagues players. His efforts, along with the work of a few others, really opened the eyes of many who had not paid attention to the injustices of those who were relegated to the Negro Leagues when they should have been part of Major League Baseball and possibly even enshrined in the Baseball Hall of Fame. It was a wonderful endeavor, and I was glad to hear all about it. After our first meeting at Mantle's, we decided to get together again soon.

We met again later in 1993, this time at P.J. Clarke's Restaurant in Manhattan. Clarke's has long been famous as a gathering place for writers, politicians, sports celebrities, and your everyday famous person. Originally it made its debut in the national consciousness for scenes in the 1945 movie *The Lost Weekend*, starring Ray Milland and Jane Wyman. The movie was nominated for seven Academy Awards and won four, including Best Picture, Best Actor, Best Adapted Screenplay, and Best Director for Billy Wilder. Personally, I liked to go to P.J. Clarke's simply because they had great burgers and it was close to where I lived.

After the usual small talk, Ed reminded me that the 25th anniversary of the 1969 Mets was coming up the next year. "What are your plans for '94?" he asked. I knew of none. He then said something very interesting. "What fee would you want for doing a baseball card show?" These events were becoming very popular. I threw out a number. Ed then asked, "What if they don't want to pay you?"

I simply said, "In that case, I wouldn't do it."

"You know," Ed said, "there is strength in numbers. What if we get the '69 Mets to unite and do signings, events, and other team-oriented things? When a group of guys sticks together and does things collectively—then you have something." It didn't take long to understand the concept. He'd hit the nail on the head. Even after a quarter century, the 1969 Mets remained incredibly popular. I couldn't stop thinking of the unbelievable possibilities for all of my teammates to capitalize on this milestone anniversary. I left the meeting excited and ready to explore this new venture. But at that point, we only knew it sounded great. We had no idea the amount of work, frustration, and disappointment we would encounter in putting this idea together!

The Art of Hitting and Joe Franklin

Before Ed Schauder and I started our efforts to bring the members of the 1969 Mets together for a 25th anniversary celebration, Ed talked me into starting the Art of Hitting. This was basically me giving hitting lessons around New York City. Ed thought this was a good way for me to stay visible and to make some extra money.

We made T-shirts and got some publicity from various events I went to. On a few occasions I went on radio or TV to talk about the Art of Hitting. It was before the internet, so there was no website to pitch; the T-shirts had a telephone number to set up classes. I didn't want to put *my* number on it, so Ed said, "All right, we'll use my number." Then Ed got me booked on *The Joe Franklin Show*. It turned out to be the final year of Joe's long career hosting his late-night TV show on Channel 9.

The Joe Franklin Show was credited with starting the talk show premise on TV. Joe sat at his desk and talked with no script, no preproduction meeting, no cue cards. It was just Joe. He was on the air, starting on what became WABC-TV in 1951—before my time in New York!—and later moving to WOR-TV in 1962. That was the same year the expansion Mets went on the air for the first time on Channel 9. If the 1962 Mets weren't ready for prime time, at least they were on when people were awake. Joe Franklin came on in the early hours of the morning and had a cult following, to put it mildly.

Joe's show wasn't fancy, and it made the *Kiner's Korner* set seem high-tech. It's worth noting that both these shows were on WOR-TV. They must have come on the air right after each other a few times over the years when a Mets game went really long because of extra innings or a rain delay. From Ralph to Joe to test pattern!

Joe's office was literally filled to the ceiling with things from his career—from promoters, from guests, from everywhere—and forever buried somewhere was a log of who was on his show and when. I couldn't find such a list, but Joe, who died in 2015, lives on thanks to YouTube. I did find out that I was one of about 300,000 guests he had on during his very long run from 1951 to 1993.

The night I was on, he also had as a guest Captain Lou Albano, a crazy character and manager in the wrestling world. He played Cyndi Lauper's father in several of her music videos. His trademark was wearing rubber bands on his ears and beard for reasons not discussed during our appearance on *The Joe Franklin Show*. To be on the same show with Captain Lou was strange, to say the least, but it was a lot of fun for my one and only time there.

Joe was his usual straitlaced self. We talked about baseball for a few minutes at his studio in Secaucus, New Jersey. I gave Joe a T-shirt for having me on the show, and he held it up for the audience. It had an immediate effect. Back in New York, the phone was ringing off the hook at Ed's place in the wee hours since the shirt had his phone number on it. Callers would think it was me and say to Ed, "Hi, Art. I want to take your class!"

It may have been low-budget and on in the middle of the night, but you can't say no one was watching Joe Franklin. After all, New York is the city that never sleeps—or stops watching TV!

Hold the Phone—and the Wedding

Ed Schauder and I had blundered using his telephone number on the air, and I had to make amends. Ed asked me to be best man at his wedding in place of his brother, who couldn't make the trip from Israel. It turned out, though, that the wedding was not a real wedding. It was staged for Ed's very religious mother, who wanted a Jewish ceremony. Ed's new wife was not Jewish, so he arranged for the whole ceremony and the party afterward just to please his mom. What a son!

Share and Share Alike

The 25th anniversary of the 1969 Mets turned out to be a labor of love. It was hard work just to try and explain to many of the players what the concept was. After many hours of conversations and calls and even some apprehension, we got everyone to buy in to the concept of a united front. Everyone understood there was strength in numbers. We had agreements for the players to sign, and most everyone did. And it turned out that even the guys who didn't sign the agreement still participated in most of the events and shared in whatever products we sold. We even made agreements with the wives of players and coaches who had passed away. That included Joan Hodges, wife of our by-then-deceased manager, Gil Hodges.

Everyone would share in licensed products from Major League Baseball. And if we were able to get personal appearances for an individual, they would keep those monies for themselves. It was a formula that worked. The goal was simple: try and get everyone to make at least $18,000 apiece, which was approximately what the players and coaches had each received from Major League Baseball for winning the World Series. Still, the process to put it together took so much time and effort that even today I'm not sure most of the players realized the effort that went into it. Trying to explain the situation all the time meant that the work for Ed and me never stopped.

We needed help. We were undermanned. Where was the old platoon system when we needed it?

The Original Mr. Met to the Rescue

We asked anyone we knew for help. One of those people was Dan Reilly, who went all the way back to the first year at Shea Stadium in 1964. Dan originally was hired for the Mets ticket office, but when he found out the team was looking for a mascot, all of a sudden he was at Shea Stadium wearing this huge Mets head. He was the very first Mr. Met!

It was just the head at first. Dan relished the job, but I'm not sure that over those first few years the enormous papier-mâché head didn't affect his general health. He wore that Mr. Met head with pride and honor, and his name became synonymous with Mets history. I knew Dan, and he offered his help, which

Ed and I gladly accepted. We even gave him a title—that kept changing. One day he would be director of marketing and the next he was vice president of sales. In some of the meetings we had with possible sponsors and various MLB-licensed companies, Dan would accompany us and actually bring his Mr. Met head with him. A few times I would look over at Dan, and he would be fast asleep. A couple of times someone asked him a question and he mumbled something; Ed and I quickly jumped in and answered. In some ways it was comedy, yet both Ed and I were grateful for his help.

A new member joined our team: Cabot Marks. Cabot had just graduated from Boston University Law School and was recommended to us by a mutual friend from the *New York Daily News*. Cabot was eager to get involved, as he wanted not only to practice business law but also to get into the world of sports management. Our efforts toward the 25th anniversary comprised a true stepping stone for him. He now has his own law firm based in New York City, and he represents a number of former athletes in business affairs and personal appearances. His help was invaluable to us.

Miracle of 1969 Enterprises

One of our big problems turned out to be the Mets themselves. Their marketing department flatly refused to let us use their logo for the proceedings; they didn't want us to take money from their sponsors for our onetime 25th anniversary celebration. This was very frustrating to us, but we decided to just develop our own logo and do the celebration on our own. That's when Miracle of 1969 Enterprises came into existence, along with its own logo.

While it wasn't the New York Mets logo, it was ours to do with as we liked. We capitalized on it and made it work. After countless meetings and phone calls, we were able to sell our concept to numerous entities, including sponsors and MLB-licensed companies. When it was all said and done, we produced 32 licensed MLB products and we got involved with a few charities, including the Muscular Dystrophy Association and Alzheimer's Association. We had baseball cards produced by Capitol Cards and others. And we were not hurting for sponsors, which included Chemical Bank, American Airlines, and the *New York Daily News*. All of them had faith in us and what we wanted to accomplish, but most of all they knew how important the 1969 Mets were and how fans would want to be around the team even after 25 years. I always ask myself, "What other team could have pulled that off?"

Floating Along on Thanksgiving

The *Daily News* was going strong at the time, and I had met John Campi, who was the head of marketing for the paper. John turned out to be a remarkable resource for us. He was the kind of person who when you said good morning to him, something clicked in his mind and he would think of a new and sometimes strange promotion for us.

John even got a number of us to ride the *Daily News* float in the 1993 Macy's Thanksgiving Day Parade, singing "(You Gotta Have) Heart"—a song we sang on our 1969 record and on *The Ed Sullivan Show* on CBS. I remember vividly sitting up front on the float next to Joan Hodges and Ed Charles. Remarkably, 24 years after the Miracle, so many thousands of people along the parade route still remembered 1969, what we accomplished, and how we affected their lives. With the 1993 Mets coming off a 103-loss season, the sight of the 100-win Miracle Mets was a holiday treat for fans.

Another person who was instrumental in our efforts at the time and who has continued to be so supportive of the 1969 Mets over the years is Andy Parton, who was with Chemical Bank and subsequently Chase Bank. Andy, an avid baseball fan, always developed events for us and remains a true fan of the 1969 Mets. He currently runs the Cradle of Aviation Museum in Garden City, Long Island. It's a wonderful place that commemorates the history of aviation, including aircraft and spacecraft.

Old-Timers' Day at Shea

Thinking about it now, one can ask, "How many teams could—25 years after accomplishing something great—have an anniversary and do all the things we did, including producing all those licensed MLB products?" It was truly "Miraculous."

As fate would have it, though, not everything worked in our favor in 1994. You might recall MLB players and ownership were having problems with a new collective bargaining agreement that had expired on December 31, 1993. On August 12, 1994, a few weeks after we took the field at Shea for Old-Timers' Day, the longest strike in baseball history began. It canceled the rest of the regular season and all postseason games, including the World Series. So the Old-Timers' event on July 17 at Shea was the last stand for baseball in 1994, and it was a beautiful day.

Bob Murphy and Ralph Kiner handled the introduction and emcee honors. You can still see the game on YouTube. They put together a top-flight team of opponents that day who we played against at Shea in 1969, including Juan Marichal, Rico Carty, Paul Blair, Curt Flood, Rick Wise, and a bunch of 1969 Cubs: Ernie Banks, Glenn Beckert, Randy Hundley, and Don Kessinger. The opposing team was managed by Earl Weaver, manager of the Orioles against us in the 1969 World Series. Shea's official scorekeeper, Red Foley, put down his pen and picked up a mic to handle the commentary with Fran Healy—and Rusty Staub and Ralph were in the dugouts doing interviews.

Earl Weaver told Rusty: "[During the '69 Series, the Orioles were] "a little nervous at the plate, but don't sell the Mets short. In retrospect, we're looking back 25 years, and two of their pitchers are in the Hall of Fame: Tom Seaver and Nolan Ryan. And then throw in Koosman and Gentry. You look back on it after all the years and all that happened, and they probably should have been the favorites."

Earl was always fun to listen to. Umpires might have thought about that differently. When he got tossed from Game 4 of the World Series, it was the first time a manager had been thrown out of a Series since Charlie Grimm in 1935. I'd known Earl since 1961, when he was the manager in Appleton, Wisconsin. The Orioles' farm club was called the Fox City Foxes in the Triple-I League—Illinois-Indiana-Iowa League, Class B. (Meanwhile, Lincoln, Nebraska, was in the league. So go figure!) It was 1961 and I was 19; Dave McNally, who started twice—and lost twice—against the Mets in the 1969 World Series, was only 18 that year with the Foxes. It was my first experience in seeing Earl and the way he managed. I could see that he was a guy who loved arguing, and he also was a guy who was going to defend his players. He turned into a great manager. Earl was voted into the Hall of Fame a couple years after he came back to Shea.

That 1994 Old-Timers' Day was the culmination of a lot of work put in by many people and a tribute to how close we all still were a quarter of a century later. This was the last Old-Timers' Day the Mets would have until 2022.

The strike lasted until April 1995. Needless to say, Miracle of '69 Enterprises hit a wall. We were moving so fast and so well, and then bam! Many fans became disillusioned with baseball, and it took a long time for the game to bounce back. We were caught in the middle and basically stopped in our tracks, but the memories of the 1969 season couldn't even be halted by a strike.

We proved that no matter how much time has gone by, the 1969 Mets are always going to be in the hearts and minds of many. Our legacy will live on forever!

Chapter 9

ISRAELI BASEBALL

How'd We End Up Here?

My first reaction was no.

Marty Appel, a longtime friend and former public relations director for the Yankees, asked me if I would be interested in managing a team in a new baseball venture in Israel starting in 2007. Marty said it would be a three-month commitment. Of course, I was aware of the problems they've had in the Middle East over the years, but honestly I was more concerned with the league being a start-up business. That was my initial apprehension, but I agreed to meet with the people setting it up. At first I just wasn't interested, but then we met a second time, and the idea started to grow on me a little bit.

I thought it would be a challenge. On top of that, I loved the idea that I could manage. It was something I'd never done. The setup seemed simple enough: wood bats, seven-inning games, designated hitter, and if the game was tied after seven, instead of extra innings, the outcome would be decided by a home-run-hitting contest. A few things started to fall into place for me, though I still did not know much about logistics, facilities, or even how the players would be chosen.

Finally, I came around to the point where I might want to give it a try. I agreed and even started to look forward to it. The organizers conducted a few tryout camps in various cities, and finally there was a player draft held at Baruch College in New York City. The last pick in the draft was a ceremonial one: Sandy Koufax, who had last pitched in the majors in 1966—the year he won his third Cy Young—and was considered by many not only to be one of the greatest pitchers ever but certainly the best Jewish pitcher in baseball history.

As for guys who would actually play in the Israel Baseball League, I met a few of them at a park near the West Side Highway for a workout. They had committed to join the start-up league. I didn't see many prospects per se, but they were eager to give organized ball a try.

Miracle in Name

The team I managed was the Modi'in Miracle. Modi'in is a relatively new city in Israel not far from Tel Aviv. Many Americans had migrated to Israel and Modi'in. It was interesting that even though we'd be representing that town, we had no association with it. The coaches and managers stayed at a nice hotel in Tel Aviv, the Dan Panorama Hotel. The players stayed in a school dorm somewhere—I'm not sure many of them liked that.

I arrived still not knowing everything that would go on with the league itself. I found out there were really only two baseball fields there. A third had to be built quickly at a park near Tel Aviv. They were grass fields, but they were not what you'd call professional grade.

The one decent field was the Baptist Village, owned by the Baptist church, believe it or not. The other was our home field at a kibbutz called Gezer—it was a converted softball field. There was a light pole in right field, which is ironic because the lights there were not good at all. (A blanket was wrapped around the pole during games to minimize the impact if an outfielder collided with it.) I think the only night games we had were at the field at the Baptist Village. The third ballpark was built in North Tel Aviv and was not very well-done.

The Gezer field, where my team played home games, was not in good shape. Right up to the first game, they were still trying to make it playable. We just had to make do. The Miracle shared the Gezer field with a team from Bet Shemesh, another small town in Israel.

Managing

A positive for me was that I knew two of the other managers. Marty Appel knew what he was doing and had three of the better-known Jewish players from our era running the teams. Former Yankee—and the first designated hitter in baseball history—Ron Blomberg managed the Bet Shemesh Blue Sox. The manager of the Petach Tikva Pioneers was Ken Holtzman, who attended my high school in St. Louis a few years after I graduated. I played against him when he was with the Cubs, and later he was briefly my teammate on the Oakland A's in 1972. He had the most wins of any Jewish pitcher in history: 174, more than Sandy Koufax (Ken beat Sandy the only time they faced each other, in 1966). Kenny left as manager after a short period because he was dissatisfied with the lousy team he had and the conditions, and he simply wasn't happy about being there.

I helped my friend Tony Ferrara get a job in the league. He knew the game and threw batting practice for both the Yankees and Mets and was a partner with me in the restaurant business. Tony had been a minor league player and was a guy who would do anything you asked him to in the game—he'd even rake and water the field if necessary. He loved being over there with me, and he really enjoyed being part of the league. He even got a chance to manage a team when Holtzman left and came back to the States. My team actually beat Tony's in the playoffs. He started as a coach on my team and an assistant to IBL commissioner Dan Kurtzer (former US ambassador to Israel and Egypt) and then managed the Petach Tikva Pioneers. It makes me laugh because two weeks before we left for Tel Aviv, he didn't even have a job in the league. He got more out of the IBL than anybody. That experience was one of the high points of his later years. He died in 2011. Tony was a good friend, and I was glad I was able to help get him the job in the IBL.

They tried to make the Miracle's uniforms look like the Mets' and Ron Blomberg's team's look like the Yankees'. They wanted to create a bit of a rivalry. We did face each other for the championship.

Players came from all over the world: Israel and the United States, obviously; Europe; Dominican Republic; Australia; Canada; a couple guys from South America—nine countries in all. Most of the players I had were not experienced enough to play professionally. The best players in the league were the Dominicans; I would classify them as third- or fourth-level players, though, again, they were clearly the best in the league. Most of them could play, because they had been playing baseball since they could walk. They just had no place to play, so they wound up in Israel.

Each team had to have three or four Israeli-born players. In some instances they were good athletes, but they didn't know the nuances of the game. I think most of the local players had recently completed their stint of mandatory military service. Every Israeli male aged 18 has to serve 32 months in the military; women serve 24 months. But the league had Israelis who were in their mid- to late 30s—the IBL needed players, and they weren't picky about who suited up.

I am not sure how they signed some of the players from other countries, but they got them to travel to Israel and stay for the season. Locating personnel was the task of Dan Duquette, former general manager of the Expos, Red Sox, and Orioles. Dan had a lot of baseball experience, but I don't know how he decided some of the players he signed were good enough to play anywhere!

Opening Day

The first game we played was against Kenny Holtzman's team. It was broadcast back to the US—on public television. That was the only game televised back home. I also agreed to call in reports to sportscaster Ed Randall for his show on WFAN.

It's hard to do a lot with a team when you have two days of practice before the league starts. (Back during our stint as entertainers in Las Vegas in the fall of 1969, Caesars Palace at least gave us *three* days of rehearsals to try to turn us ballplayers into singers.) In Israel there were no good practice facilities. We also didn't have a lot of equipment, so we tried not to lose baseballs and not to break bats.

It was certainly hot there, but it was summer. It got very crowded in August, when Europe closes down. Europeans take the whole month off, the continent empties out, and they like to vacation in places with great beaches. The Europeans didn't go to Israel for the baseball, I learned.

Anthems and Prayers

Before games, they played two national anthems: Israeli and American. We kept our hats on during the Israeli anthem but took them off for our national anthem.

We couldn't play Friday night or Saturday during the day because of the Jewish Sabbath. One day we had a long game on a Friday afternoon, and we heard an announcement that they were going to conduct a prayer service behind the stands. One of my Dominican pitchers came up to me and asked in broken English if he could go to the prayer service. "I'm not sure this is the kind of prayer service you want to go to," I told him, "but sure." He wasn't pitching that day, so I told him in broken Spanish to go to the service and come right back. A couple minutes later, he was back.

"What happened?" I asked him.

"No entiendo," he told me. Which meant he didn't understand anything they said or did in the service for getting ready for the Sabbath.

I felt bad for the Dominican players. This was a whole new world for them with the cultural differences there. I don't know if they found places to enjoy food. The American players, whose grumblings I could understand, complained about the food at the dorm. I can only imagine what the Dominicans said about the cuisine in Spanish. A lot of them were so eager to play, they let a lot of issues roll off their backs.

I told the team before the first game that this place was where history was made many years before, and the reality was they were there to play baseball, and they never knew who was watching them. That's the same thing I tell kids in clinics I do in the States; maybe someone knows somebody who knows somebody who's in the stands. I told my team in Israel that no matter what the conditions were, it was a professional league and they were to conduct themselves in a professional manner and give 100 percent every minute they were out there.

A couple of the players from the IBL did get signed to MLB minor league contracts. One of my players, the league co-MVP Eladio Rodriguez, played in the minor leagues the following season. He had been a catcher in the Red Sox system for a few years before landing in Israel. He impressed some people and was signed after the season as a catcher in the minors with the Yankees. The organization had some injuries, and he made it all the way to Triple A in 2008.

Napkins and Big Guys

The umpiring was relatively bad—I don't know where they got the umpires. We didn't really even have lineup cards. Sometimes we wrote the lineups on bits of cardboard; other times we got more inventive. Ron Blomberg, who calls everybody "big guy," handed in a napkin as a lineup card, with every player listed as Big Guy. I had some lineup cards that one of the managers brought from Australia. So we handed in our lineups to the umps, and one read "New South Wales Baseball League" and the other was a napkin.

I protested one IBL game and got a letter from the commissioner denying it. The protest was about the home-run-hitting

contest to decide a tie game; I was informed that the player in
the contest from the other team used an illegal bat—a combination of wood and something else. I was also ejected from a
game for protesting a call at second base where the runner slid
in and knocked the glove off my fielder. The umpire called him
out and then changed his mind and called him safe. I fired out
a few bad words, and he kicked me out. The weird thing was
there was nowhere to go once I got kicked out of the game.
There was no clubhouse or anyplace to retreat to, so I just kind
of hung around.

So in my one year managing in Israel, I protested one
game, I was kicked out of one game, and I made it to the
championship game. I lost all three! The biggest regret—or
you might say curse—was losing to Ron Blomberg's team in
the championship game when he didn't know the name of
a single player on his team. Ronnie had a really good coach
who helped make up the lineup and set the strategy for the
team.

Ron and I would work out early in the morning at a gym
at the hotel where we stayed. We'd go right from there to
the wonderful buffet breakfast at the Dan Panorama. Ron is
a big eater, so we'd go over to the breakfast buffet and he'd
have all sorts of different things: bread, eggs, whatever kind
of meats they cooked that day—I mean, just a pile of food all
around him. Once, as he was scarfing up this big breakfast,
he looked up at me and asked, "Hey, big guy, where do you
want to go for dinner tonight?" It was 8:30 in the morning!
We both had a game coming up in a few hours, but all he
wanted to know was where we were eating that night. I guess
he was concerned because he was a meat-and-potatoes guy
and he was not crazy about the food over there. Not that you
would have known judging by the piles of his food casting

shadows on the table. Ronnie was really funny and a great person to spend all that time with. The big guy made it work.

A few weeks after the IBL season was over and we were back in the States, I called Ron. While we were catching up, I asked him to name five players on his IBL team. He said, "Sure. I had the big guy at first base, the big guy at shortstop, the big guy in right field, the big guy catching, and the big guy as the DH." I just smiled and shook my head.

The Beginning of Something

As I look back, it was a wonderful experience for me. I took managing very seriously. I tried to find Gil Hodges's managing style: know every player on my team, be aware of their strengths and weaknesses, and be fair in what I did. However, I was frustrated by the quality of play and the playing conditions. I had experience as a big-league player, and I expected things to be at a certain level of professionalism. The Israelis on my team were eager to learn, but they didn't know the nuances of the game. It's a game you need to be familiar with from an early age to know what to do and how to react. Some of the Israelis in the league could run or show a little power, but they really didn't know what to do when the ball came to them in the field.

The people were very friendly. To be honest, though, they didn't know much about the game either. At the time, basketball was the big sport in Israel. And soccer was very popular, as was tennis. The managers and some coaches dressed at the hotel because there were no locker facilities at the fields. When we all met in the lobby in uniform, many people looked at us like we were in some kind of a show. The players took buses from where they were staying. Managers went by car or van to one of the three parks. One time the van didn't come to pick us up after a game at Yarkon Park in Tel Aviv. So we had to walk to the main road to try to catch a cab. No cars stopped, but we got plenty of stares as we stood on the corner in our uniforms. People drove by, looking at us, honking their horns at our outfits. I think people thought we were some sort of clown group.

The league had financial difficulties and folded after that one season, but I think the IBL in 2007 was a precursor to Israel taking baseball more seriously. The Israel Association of Baseball really started to develop the game after that. One of the big problems during my time there was the fields—namely that there really weren't any, even for kids' leagues. Since 2007 they have focused on developing the game and have built more and better fields. Since the IBL folded, Israel has done well in the World Baseball Classic and the Olympics. I think Ron Blomberg, Kenny Holtzman, and I really laid the groundwork for Israel to become a presence in international baseball.

I still frequently get asked about my time in Israel and the beginning of the IBL. I met some wonderful people, and I learned a lot about the problems on both sides of the dilemma over there. It was worth learning how people live with constant threats. Everyone was on guard there; all restaurants had security guards in front who would pat you down and check purses and bags. There weren't many metal detectors; checks were mostly done by Israeli service people. I realized once people got to know you and like you, it was like being in Italy or Spain or any other country that welcomes Americans.

I enjoyed my time in Israel. I tried to teach everyone there what I knew. It turned out to be a wonderful experience. I found it to be a real challenge, but I enjoyed it. I really loved managing. And I loved the DH, which was kind of surprising. I have been back to Israel to do baseball clinics. The time there brought me back into the game. And for that, I'll always be grateful. And as I mentioned earlier, I truly believe that those of us who were there in 2007 were the catalysts to grow the game of baseball there.

Chapter 10

LEGACY

1969 vs. 1986

In their first 60-plus years as a franchise, the Mets only secured two world championships, so to be a part of one of them is very special. All of us share that and are very much aware of it. I do have to say that I was disappointed that only four guys from the 1969 team were invited to Old-Timers' Day in 2022. It was such a great event, but I felt like there should have been more representation from 1969.

It is great to see all those guys who were part of the 1986 team at events around the city and at Citi Field. I know all those guys, from Mookie Wilson to Tim Teufel to Darryl Strawberry to Dwight Gooden to Keith Hernandez to Ron Darling. I've become friendly with them all. And I think they look at me as someone who is involved in the history of the Mets. It's a common ground that we share, and it's something we are all proud of.

It was wonderful to see Doc and Darryl getting their uniform numbers retired—along with Keith a couple of years ago. The '69 Mets have good representation in the row of retired numbers atop Citi Field too, with Tom Seaver, Jerry Koosman, and Gil Hodges.

The only Met who was in uniform for both world championships was Bud Harrelson, catalyst of the 1969 infield and third-base coach for the 1986 team. Tom Seaver was also in uniform, but it was a Red Sox uniform, so that isn't quite the same. Tom was injured and had already thrown what would end up being his last pitch in the major leagues by 1986.

I look at the 1986 team as a really exciting club. I look at the 1969 Mets as being the Miracle team. The '86 team had a lot expected of them, based on what they did in 1985, making it to the last weekend and being edged out by the Cardinals. They were expected to win in '86, and they did. Whereas we came from nowhere, and everyone expected us to be in last place in 1969—that truly is the Miracle.

That's not to take anything away from the 1986 team. They were a come-from-behind team in that year's postseason. They could have lost four in a row to Houston in the playoffs, but they didn't. Everybody knows what happened in '86: they rallied and had a lot of clutch hitting. The 1969 and 1986 groups were different teams from different times that ended up in the same place: dancing around the mound at Shea Stadium.

Keith Hernandez

Keith Hernandez is a friend and a very good guy. Keith was drafted by the Cardinals and had his first spring training the same year I went to camp with St. Louis in 1972. He was 18 and fresh out of high school that spring—he didn't even have his mustache yet. Keith made his major league debut with St. Louis a couple years after I was there.

I mostly know Keith from being around New York. Because he was coming up when I was near the end of my career, I think of him more as a friend than as a ballplayer contemporary—though, of course, he was a great hitter and a brilliant fielder, and he has been a beloved announcer with the team for a long time. I don't often watch or listen to the games, but I know he's excellent with Ron Darling and Gary Cohen. They're all very good in the booth.

Keith came to New York a couple of years after I was a broadcaster for the Mets. He was already a star, an MVP, a batting champion, a perennial Gold Glove first baseman, and a World Series hero from the previous year with the Cardinals, but he had run afoul of Whitey Herzog and been shipped to the Mets. Keith has said that in 1983 he thought of Shea Stadium as "Baseball Siberia." He was thrust into a leadership role on a young team.

Some guys are kind of thrown into a situation like that and deal with it, some don't want that kind of responsibility, and others cherish the moment they are able to be in that position. I've seen the full spectrum of that: guys you'd think would want to be team leaders, but they take a step back and just be who they are; others want the responsibility, the notoriety, and the challenge. Keith was the true leader of the team that culminated in the 1986 world championship.

I'm not sure we had anybody quite like a Keith figure in 1969. We had a general group of guys on that team—I don't think you'd call them all followers, but I don't know that you would say anyone was the leader of that team. Maybe the closest we had in terms of an everyday player filling that role was Donn Clendenon after he came over from Montreal in June 1969. As I mentioned a few times, Donn was the kind of guy who would get on you—and Kenny Boswell and I were no exceptions. He turned out to be a lawyer later in life, and he always was a clubhouse lawyer in the wildest sense of the word. Then there was Ed "the Glider" Charles; he didn't say much, but he led through his demeanor and his experience. Tom Seaver? He led by his brilliance on the mound—as did Jerry Koosman.

Keith earned the honor of being the first Met to wear a *C* on his uniform as captain. And over the years I've done some things with his charity that benefits Alzheimer's—he even shaved his trademark mustache outside Citi Field for a $10,000 donation to an adult day health center in Brooklyn a decade ago. If A's owner Charlie Finley were still with us, he'd be amazed at the inflation for mustache donation!

Mookie

Another guy I am friends with from the 1986 club is Mookie Wilson. I have known him since his days in the minor leagues. When I was working with Channel 5, I did a *Sports Extra* special in 1980 about Mookie that was called "One Step Away." It was about Mookie preparing to come up to the majors as an exciting young player. It also featured a veteran relief pitcher in his mid-30s who was on his way to the minors, Dyar Miller.

We filmed it down in Tidewater at the Mets' Triple A facility on the Virginia coast. Mookie was a really sweet guy—and always has been. I met his wife and his family. I still see him at Mets events all the time. Having known him since he was a minor leaguer, and having spent a good amount of time with him at Tidewater and doing reporting after he made the step up to Shea, it is wonderful to see how much success he has had. He remains as sincere as he was as a kid in the minors from a small town in South Carolina.

Announced as Pinch-Hitter at Agee Wedding

Tommie Agee's wedding to his wife, Maxcine, was a beautiful affair in Yonkers in 1985. I was part of the wedding party. Mudcat Grant was there, plus a few other ballplayers. There was one player who was conspicuously late, though: Tommie's childhood friend in Alabama and teammate in New York, Cleon Jones. Cleon was the best man. He wasn't there as the hour for the service approached. I was minding my own business, getting ready for the ceremony, when Maxcine came up to me and said, "You might have to fill in for Cleon as best man."

"Where's Cleon?" I asked.

"He's not here yet. We have to get started. They have another wedding scheduled."

It was down to the wire in terms of time, and Cleon came through like he did as a player—delivering in the late innings when you started to lose hope. He finally showed up, and they were able to go through the ceremony. I was called back to the line of ushers and resumed my place with them. All Cleon said was, "I knew you wouldn't start until I got there." Cleon, his wife, and his family had stopped for breakfast. I'm not sure if he didn't know what time the wedding started or if he was just hungry. We went through with the ceremony just about as scheduled.

Cleon is such a fantastic guy, but he usually goes at his own pace. He got there when he got there, and he wasn't too late. But he was not going to miss breakfast.

Brooks and Palmer

I got to know Brooks Robinson pretty well over the years. We lost one of the great ballplayers and people in the sport when he passed in 2023. The Hall of Fame third baseman made some great plays against us in the World Series in '69, but the 1970 Series belonged to him. I can still hear Curt Gowdy yelling after he robbed Red after Red in that World Series: "This guy is in another world. He's unbelievable!" Brooks was MVP of that Series for his glove, but he also batted .429 with two homers. If you add in the damage he did as Baltimore swept the Twins in the ALCS, he hit .485 and drove in eight runs in as many postseason games. Sixteen Gold Gloves—all of them earned. How lucky was I to have played with and against all these unbelievably great players in that era?

Brooks was a founding member of the Major League Baseball Players Alumni Association. I played golf with him a lot at the Joe DiMaggio Children's Hospital Foundation charity event in Fort Lauderdale, the same city where the Orioles trained for years. Brooks was forever involved with Baltimore, working for the team as a broadcaster and at countless charity events—and the last day at old Memorial Stadium would not have been complete without Brooks and Colts quarterback Johnny Unitas throwing out first pitches.

Brooks was a terrific person, but he never forgave us for winning that 1969 World Series. Neither did Jim Palmer.

Palmer, the Hall of Fame Orioles pitcher we beat in Game 3, always told me that the Orioles from the mid-1960s to the mid-1970s would be ranked among the greatest teams of all time if not for losing that Series to the Mets. Well, Jim, you'll have to settle for being *one* of the greatest teams of the era: five division titles, four pennants, and two world championships from 1966 to 1974.

The Hand of DiMaggio

The first time I met Joe DiMaggio was in spring training early in my career. We were in Bradenton, Florida, and had just ridden over from the Reds' camp in Tampa. We got off the bus and were walking over to the dugout in the Kansas City A's spring facility. DiMaggio was there, standing behind the batting cage and watching us walk in. I was with a group of the big-name players—Frank Robinson, Vada Pinson, and Pete Rose are the ones I recall.

Robby, Vada, and Pete all stopped to say hello to DiMaggio. I was the unknown young guy in a small group of four or five people, and I didn't feel like I belonged. DiMaggio went down the line shaking hands:

"Hey, Frank, how are you doing?"

"Hello, Vada. Sure. Good to see you."

"Pete. I know you. Mr. Hustle, Charlie Hustle."

And I was right there at the end. I stuck out my hand and said, "Hi, Mr. DiMaggio. Art Shamsky. Honored to meet you."

He said some pleasantry to me, but I was in a trance. As soon as he shook my hand, I thought of his hand and Marilyn Monroe. Then I said to myself, "I'm never ever going to wash my right hand." It's amazing what comes to your mind sometimes.

The Natural Minus Two Mets

My friend Tony Ferrara was the technical director for the movie *The Natural* in 1984. Robert Redford starred in the movie, and a lot of the baseball scenes were filmed at War Memorial Stadium in Buffalo. They asked me to try out for it, but I was running a restaurant. Tony was on location in Buffalo for a couple of months, and it would have been difficult for me to be away from the business for that long.

Eddie Kranepool was invited and begged off too. Ed wrote about it in his book, *The Last Miracle*: "I'd lived in Buffalo before when I was in the minors and I wasn't particularly fond of the town. I wasn't looking forward to spending six weeks or more in a place I wasn't fond of."

My first minor league stop was Geneva, New York, and I enjoyed it, so I am going to lay off Buffalo. I will say *The Natural* was pretty successful when it came out. I guess we missed our big shot at the big screen—and Buffalo.

How Do You Get to Carnegie Hall?

There's the old joke where a tourist asks a man on a New York street, "How do you get to Carnegie Hall?" The man replies, "Practice."

When Rudy Giuliani was mayor of New York in the 1990s, he put together a special baseball event at Carnegie Hall. He asked a few '69 Mets to take part. There was a rehearsal earlier on the day of the show, but I was the only one who went to it. The other players lived out of Manhattan, so I was the only one close by during the day. There I was, the lone ballplayer at rehearsal singing with Skitch Henderson and the New York Pops orchestra. I played at a lot of big stadiums and batted in the World Series with millions of eyes on me, but I never felt as out of place as I did that day. There were just enough people in the audience at rehearsal to make my singing more nerve-racking. All I could think during that rehearsal was, *God, I hope the other guys show up tonight for the real performance.*

That was a trip, and thankfully the guys made it in time to perform in front of a full house. Rudy came onstage, we all sang, and it was a fun night. At least I can always say I performed at Carnegie Hall!

Everybody Loves Shamsky

I have a number of people who have named their dogs after me, including the comedian Jon Stewart. People come up to me and ask me about the dog on the show *Everybody Loves Raymond* being named after me. The dog and my name were mentioned a lot, and I—along with some of my '69 Mets teammates—appeared on an episode in 1999. To this day people continue to wonder if I know about the dog being named after me. Let me put it on paper here for all to see: yes, I know about the dog and the show!

I even know the backstory of how the dog came to be. Raymond (played by Ray Romano) found the dog and gave it to his brother, Robert (Brad Garrett).

It turns out the executive producer of the show, Phil Rosenthal, grew up in Flushing, near Shea Stadium. He was a Mets fan and a fan of mine. Someone from the show tracked down my mom and called her. They asked her if she had some memorabilia she wanted to put up on a wall on the set. My mom, who was not the most knowledgeable baseball fan, said, "Let me see what I've got." She called me, and I told her, "Don't send them anything. Let me talk to them."

I talked to Phil Rosenthal, who said, "We can't pay anything because it's a parody. Like a skit on *Saturday Night Live*." Phil and I talked for a bit, and he said, "Let's do something on the show. Maybe we can develop it and get a few other players on."

So we had eight Mets on *Everybody Loves Raymond*. The episode, titled "Big Shots," included 1969 Mets Ed Kranepool, Tug McGraw, Ron Swoboda, Bud Harrelson, Cleon Jones,

Tommie Agee, Jerry Grote, and me. We had a lot of fun. We did receive a fee for initially being on the show, and they flew us out to Warner Bros. Studios in Burbank, California. We've gotten residual checks over the years, but because the reruns are on cable TV, those residual checks don't amount to a lot of money. I have actually gotten one or two checks where the amount was in pennies. So don't think we are getting rich off the residuals. But as I said, it was a lot of fun.

The episode plays out like this: The set is supposed to be the Hall of Fame in Cooperstown. Ray and Robert have come to meet members of the Miracle Mets, who are doing a signing. They want me to sign the dog's collar. Ray—who plays a *Newsday* sports columnist on the show—won't wait in line, and he tries to push his way to the front. Tug had most of the lines. My big line is, "I'm Art Shamsky. I'll take care of this," as we try to get seated at a diner toward the end of the episode.

The production really gave me great admiration for the people who do these shows—especially with a live audience. They have to get some laughs, then they have to reshoot, and then they have to get some more laughs. I watch *Everybody Loves Raymond* almost every day now. It's constantly on in syndication somewhere. No matter what kind of day you've had, it makes you feel like everything's going to be fine. I'm so glad to have been a part of it. And judging by all the dog questions I get every time I make an appearance, a lot of people watch the reruns. It does keep my name out there.

The Magnificent Seasons

The force that pushed me onward for my book *The Magnificent Seasons*—besides the adulation I saw when people waited in line for hours to talk for a moment about that time—was that all three teams I wrote about won for the first time in 1969–70. A lot of people thought the Knicks had won a championship previously, but they hadn't. The Mets and Jets were still considered new franchises. The Jets had one winning season before their championship season, while the Mets hadn't even come close. I thought the way to do the book was to talk about those teams and also what was going on in the world at the time: the war in Vietnam, the assassinations, the riots. There was a lot of disruption in the world—not unlike what is going on now: problems at universities, unrest, and serious political divisions. That three teams from the same city won in the midst of all this—I knew that was a story.

What happened during those 18 months in 1969–70 remains so relevant all these years later. I thought there had to be a way to write about all three teams and tie them together in one book. I talked it over with a few people and met Barry Zeman, who ended up writing it with me. Then there was interest from Thomas Dunne Books, a subsidiary of St. Martin's Press.

I conducted more than 100 interviews and was constantly at the New York Public Library searching out newsworthy events to accompany what was happening in sports at that time. I looked in a lot of different periodicals, and I could never find any good news. There was nothing but bad news—except for in the world of sports. The Jets, the Mets, and the Knicks gave the city a lift that it really needed. I can tell you from personal experience that people have still not forgotten.

I talked to so many people and related so many stories, but one interview I'll mention is from an unsung Mets hero who didn't make a catch, throw a pitch, or swing a bat in 1969: Pete Flynn. The longtime Shea groundskeeper slept at the stadium along with the crew during the final weeks of the season, working all hours to repair a field torn apart after each of our three clinchings: for the division, pennant, and World Series. After the Series, the crew had to not only repair the field but convert it to football so the Jets could play there until winter. Flynn said, "I'm just glad the 1969–70 Knicks didn't play at Shea."

Leading Cardinal

Cardinal Timothy Dolan, archbishop of New York, grew up in St. Louis, like I did. When I first met him, he recognized my name. He said, "Of course I know you. So Art, what's wrong with the Cardinals?" I wasn't sure he was talking about the baseball team in St. Louis or the cardinals at the Vatican.

"You grew up in St. Louis," he said. "I imagine you were a St. Louis Cardinals fan. I was a big fan. Stan the Man was my hero."

I told him Stan Musial was my hero too. "I couldn't go to bed as a kid without listening to his last at-bat," I confessed.

Just like Cardinal Dolan, who is a handful of years younger than me, I idolized a lot of those Cardinals growing up in St. Louis. I watched them on television—the kind of black-and-white TV with the rabbit ears. I grew up with announcers Harry Caray, Jack Buck, and Joe Garagiola in St. Louis. The Cardinals always had a good team, and that's how I became indoctrinated.

Cardinal Dolan is a wonderful person. I've been friends with him since he came to New York in 2009. I cherish that friendship. And we have that common bond that we both grew up fans of the Cardinals and idolized Stan "the Man" Musial. Whether you become a cardinal—or even a Met—where you grew up and the team you grew up with always has a special place in your heart.

The Last Day at Shea

Tom Seaver threw out the final pitch. I thought that was very appropriate. Who caught the ball? Mike Piazza. Nothing against Piazza—he's one of the all-time great Mets—but that day in 2008, Gary Carter was standing not far away watching it all. Gary was the only player from the '86 team enshrined in the Hall of Fame at Cooperstown. His hit at Shea started the winning rally from two runs down with two outs and no one on in the 10th inning of Game 6 of the World Series against the Red Sox. He caught the last strike of the last world championship at Shea.

I understand from a marketing standpoint that the Mets wanted a more current name. Maybe the organization was signaling that it wanted Mike to go into the Hall of Fame as a Met rather than as a Dodger. Against Carter's wishes, the Hall of Fame had decided to put an Expos logo on his plaque. When Piazza was inducted in Cooperstown several years later, the Hall of Fame put a Mets hat on his plaque. But when Shea closed in 2008, Piazza had just retired. Only one person could catch the ceremonial last pitch from Seaver, the unquestioned greatest Met ever. Mike was a tremendous player; I just thought it was strange it wasn't Gary catching that last pitch.

The ceremony on September 28, 2008, was the culmination of a long, dreary day with a rain delay and the final out that eliminated the Mets from postseason contention on the last day of the season. The Mets could have held the ceremony before the game, but they waited until after the game. Another weird choice, but the team went out of its way to bring many former

Mets to the ballpark and gave them the same uniforms they wore during their playing days. It was an honor standing on that field with the fans still cheering until the end.

Forty or so former Mets were on hand, including my 1969 teammates Ed Charles, Wayne Garrett, Bud Harrelson, Al Jackson, Cleon Jones, Jerry Koosman, Ed Kranepool, Ron Swoboda, Seaver, and me. The players all lined up and walked down each line—one person at a time—to make a farewell gesture at home plate. I remember bending over to touch home. I have a very special photo of that moment.

It was a bittersweet day. I understand progress, I understand the bottom line, and I understand Shea had gotten old. In order to compete with other franchises, other cities, and other venues, things have to be newer and better. I get it. When Shea opened in 1964, it replaced one of the grand old stadiums, the Polo Grounds. The old gives way to the new. But Shea will always be a very special part of my life. The day it was torn down, part of my youth was taken from me. I still think about that.

I get a lot of questions from fans about Shea Stadium as compared to Citi Field. I like Citi Field. It's beautiful. But I loved Shea. I loved the playing field itself. You could see the ball well at the plate and in the outfield. The planes overhead never bothered me. It held so many people. The ballpark was just right. Shea may have gotten beaten up over the years, but it had history.

Shea was where I made a name for myself and where I was part of this incredible team, this incredible year. I still think about something that happened at Shea every day.

After the Miracle

I always enjoyed writing. When we decided to set the wheels in motion that resulted in my book *After the Miracle*, fate was with us.

My cowriter, Erik Sherman, and I arranged for the two of us—along with Jerry Koosman, Ron Swoboda, and Bud Harrelson—to reunite with Tom Seaver at his vineyard in Tom's native California. Erik and I had done a number of interviews, but I didn't want to do one on the phone with Tom. It was important that we be face-to-face. Separate from that, Tom had recently announced that he was having cognitive issues, which began after a severe case of Lyme disease. I thought that if we could get Buddy Harrelson to go, it would be therapeutic for both of them. Part of the story would be coming out to see a teammate who was not well, and bringing out his roommate and good friend who at the time was in a similar situation health-wise.

No matter what happened during that long weekend in May 2017, it could not change that we were all friends of Tom's who had achieved something remarkable together at a young age. Time can't dim the accomplishment.

With everyone's schedules, health, and five people traveling from all over the country, we really had limited time to get together at Tom and Nancy Seaver's vineyard in Northern California. Though there were some difficulties in the end, it worked out beautifully. We got to tell stories and reminisce with our Hall of Fame teammate. Sharing it with Buddy gave the book, in my mind, so much more meaning. He was Tom's roommate for a decade, a fellow Californian, and the glue of that team. He was a little guy who was kind, gave everything he had, and wasn't afraid to take on Pete Rose—or anyone else.

The last part of that book is about friendships and remembrances—standing with our friend who had just announced he was not well and was no longer traveling, and having brought his friend who also was not well to see him, maybe for the last time. We didn't even know if we'd actually be able to see Seaver until that Saturday morning.

When we got to California on Friday after all of us connecting in San Francisco, we spoke to Nancy. She said Tom was not doing well that day. "Let's try tomorrow," she advised. My first thought was that Saturday was the only day we could do it. We would be an hour away from the San Francisco International Airport, and we all had long flights that included time and logistics constraints.

Once again Seaver was right: God was a Mets fan. It turned out Tom was feeling better on Saturday, and we rushed to get to his home. Yes, the Mets fan above brought us together that Saturday. It turned out to be a glorious day. It was also sad in some ways. I don't want to take away from that special day, because we spent about eight hours together, sharing moments and memories. We toured Tom's pride-and-joy vineyard in Calistoga, we laughed, we joked, and maybe a couple of us cried. In some ways I wish the whole team could have been there. In other ways it felt like they were.

It was bittersweet at the end of the day, because we just didn't know what would happen in the coming months. And when we said goodbye, it was sad. A lot of it goes back to us not being a good team in 1968. Friendships aside, for a team that finished ninth a year earlier to go through this incredible season was astounding. Buddy and Ron had been through the bad times with the team in '65—not as far back as Eddie

Kranepool went, but they saw a couple of 100-loss seasons and were part of the Lovable Losers. Ron even had some run-ins with Casey Stengel, who was in his final year as a manager before breaking his hip and having to retire. Seaver came later— he was the ray of hope on a team that had lost 101 games in 1967 as he was winning Rookie of the Year. Jerry and I both arrived on the scene in '68—Koo from the minors and me from Cincinnati—and we didn't see the really low times.

That day in Seaver Vineyards was an incredibly wonderful, bittersweet journey—one last day with Tom. Part of the beauty of the book was the trip out and sharing the wonderful moments while flying to San Francisco, driving to Napa, spending time together at the hotel, and all of us with the shared experience of Tom and Nancy's home and what they'd done with that piece of land. Tom went into the wine business after the kind of baseball life you could only dream of: star pitcher, pitchman, broadcaster, and someone who stood for something. He was so focused, always looking forward, and then being granted that short window when he was able to look back and share it all again with us was simply a gift. I was so glad to be able to share something that special and unique. Those memories will last forever!

50th Anniversary with My Buddy

For the 50th anniversary of the 1969 Mets at Citi Field in 2019, we were in golf carts that had seats on the back facing out, so we could wave to the crowd and they could have a better look at us. We went out from left field, two of us at a time, except for Ed Kranepool; he was alone at the end and gave the address to the crowd. Ed had been through a lot with a kidney transplant, and he did a tremendous job with his speech. It was really the first reunion where Tom Seaver couldn't make it and serve as spokesman, but like a guy who is among the all-time elite pinch-hitters in history, Steady Eddie came through in the clutch.

I was on the cart with Buddy Harrelson. At that point, Buddy was in a bad way. He had dementia and was perhaps 80 percent not really there. I had to put my arm on him so he wouldn't fall out of the cart. That experience for me was heartbreaking, but it was also exhilarating. I saw the love people had, mostly for Buddy—everybody knew what was going on with him. It was really a breathtaking moment.

As we rode in, Howie Rose—as always, serving as emcee—told a wonderful story: "About 10 years ago, Buddy Harrelson said that when he would meet any of his former teammates at events like this, he'd shake their hand. But then as he saw old teammates begin to pass, he said, 'You know what, I'm giving them all a hug.'" The cheering started to build again, and Howie went on, "Well, Buddy, you just got a great big hug from 40,000 people!"

Now Batting for Kranepool

I have done a lot of speaking engagements, but one of the biggest thrills for me was when I spoke from the pulpit at St. Patrick's Cathedral on behalf of Ed Kranepool in 2022. The 25th Annual Remember & Rejoice Service was an outpouring of appreciation and altruism on each side of the aisle. On one side of the church were people who had received transplants and their families, and on the other side were donors and their loved ones.

It was especially stirring with the bagpipes echoing, along with the fact that the event hadn't been held in a couple of years due to COVID. No doubt many of the people present had endured serious issues because of added health risks during the pandemic. What a thrill to be there thanking them and recognizing the donation of a kidney to Eddie.

Ed had been getting around with a special cane that bore the Mets logo, which had been a gift to him from Teresa Taylor, who had a Major League Baseball license to use the Mets logo for canes and bandages. She had previously given a cane with the Mets logo to Rubén Tejada after his leg was broken on a slide at second base by Chase Utley of the Dodgers during the 2015 Division Series. (The next day the papers erroneously said Mets ownership had given Tejada the cane; consider this note a clarification.) Ed couldn't attend the St. Patrick's event in 2022 due to a health issue. Old friend Marty Appel, who was involved in setting up the program at St. Patrick's, arranged for me to step in and represent him.

It felt like Eddie was in the pulpit with me. I thought about my favorite moment of his remarkable career as the longest-serving Met in history. It was October 14, 1969, when he blasted a drive over the wall in center to cap off the Game 3 victory in the first World Series game at Shea Stadium—the day Tommie Agee made those two incredible catches and also homered as we took the lead in the Series against the heavily favored Orioles. I could picture Ed rounding the bases as his baseball life reached full circle: Lovable Loser to Miracle Met. He was signed by the team during its first year in 1962, going from high school to the Polo Grounds—with a few minor league stops thrown in—and getting his first hit in the majors all while he was still 17.

And then in 2019, suffering badly from the effects of Type 2 diabetes and in need of a kidney transplant, word came that there was a matching donor at Stony Brook University Hospital.

Like I said in my brief speech at St. Patrick's, "Miracles do happen. And it's only because of the goodness and humanity of donors and families like you who have given the precious gift of life so that others might live on." Ed had a life well lived. I'm glad and proud to have been his friend and teammate.

24

Old-Timers' Day a couple of years ago was great. The climactic moment was when the Mets unveiled number 24 on top of Citi Field and announced that my number had been retired—for Willie Mays. Yes, I wore that number before Willie, and it has only been worn a handful of times since. The Mets didn't give me a heads-up before I was standing on the field watching the unveiling with everyone else. I was at Citi Field, but unfortunately Willie's health didn't allow him to travel for the event.

But I am the only 24 to take part in a Mets victory parade. Willie and I both wore it in a World Series—me in 1969 and him in 1973—though the Mets lost that '73 Series to the Oakland A's in seven games. My 24 uniform was drenched in champagne at Shea after we won the '69 Series. And speaking of that, I can't for the life of me figure out why I didn't take home the uniform I wore in the 1969 Series. Several other guys did, and those uniforms are now incredible keepsakes and valuable collector's items. Ken Boswell and I just threw our uniforms on the floor for the clubhouse guys to wash—like it was any other game.

I wonder what the team would have done if I had been on the Mets when Willie Mays arrived in 1972. Would they have asked me for my number, or would they have just taken it from me? I think that would have been tough for me, if they'd done that without even talking to me.

Of course, Willie is one of the all-time greatest players, and I certainly would have tried to accommodate him. But if the team took the number without asking me, I think that would have gotten me upset. But it's all a moot point—I was no longer on the Mets by the time they finally got Willie in May 1972. The Mets had tried to get him from the Giants for years because Mets owner Mrs. Payson, a former Giants shareholder, loved him so much and he was such a star. First baseman/pinch-hitter Jim Beauchamp had number 24 when Willie arrived. I don't know any locker room particulars, but I can imagine the hanger with that jersey on it moved pretty quickly from the locker of someone with one month as a Met to the Say Hey Kid's stall.

I was traded to St. Louis for Beauchamp in October 1971. That uniform must have fit Jim best, because a lot of people were in that deal. I went to St. Louis along with Jim Bibby, who would go on to throw a no-hitter and was an All-Star with a long career, plus pitchers Rich Folkers and Charlie Hudson. The Cardinals sent back Beauchamp, Chuck Taylor, Chip Coulter, and Harry Parker, a relief pitcher who performed well during the Mets' 1973 pennant drive.

Number 24 was *unofficially* retired after Willie called it quits in 1973. He then wore it as a Mets coach from 1974 through 1979. Rickey Henderson and Robinson Cano later wore the number—with Willie's blessing. First baseman Kelvin Torve was assigned that number for a few days in 1990; after the fans and media went ballistic, Torve was quickly given number 39.

Let the record show that I wore it longer than anyone as a Mets player. Here is a list of all the 24s and how long they wore it, courtesy of the websites Mets by the Numbers and Ultimate Mets Database.

Number 24		First Worn	Last Worn
1	Bob Miller	04/21/1962	09/29/1962
2	Johnny Lewis	04/12/1965	06/11/1967
3	Ed Charles	05/12/1967	05/22/1967
4	Ken Boswell	09/18/1967	10/01/1967
5	**Art Shamsky**	04/10/1968	09/25/1971
6	Jim Beauchamp	04/23/1972	05/10/1972
7	Willie Mays	05/14/1972	10/16/1973
8	Kelvin Torve	08/07/1990	08/17/1990
9	Rickey Henderson	04/05/1999	05/13/2000
10	Robinson Cano	03/28/2019	05/08/2022

Number Retired: 08/27/2022

Podcast

I was never more thankful for my health than during the COVID-19 pandemic, but the extra time at home during the lockdown gave me an itch to try something new. I joined the seemingly endless array of people doing podcasts. I wanted to push myself and keep all my synapses firing, so I extended my podcast beyond sports.

One of my first guests was Joe Namath—we both struggled with Zoom. We reminisced about 1969 and had some laughs about New York in the late 1960s. He was such a giant sports hero, and still is. To me it was a thrill to do the show with him.

My last guest was Ken Burns, producer of many great PBS documentary series. Ken's so talented. Not only with sports but with all history and so many other subjects: war, music, literature, race, biography, nature, famine, depression, government. He can—and does—just keeping going on. We had something in common, though. Both the project in 1994 for the 25th anniversary of the 1969 world championship and his great documentary on PBS, *Baseball,* were affected by the baseball strike. Baseball didn't come back until spring the following year. It was the longest work stoppage in the game's history.

Pete Rose was a great guest, and it didn't hurt that we knew each other since we were 18. Well, technically he was 19, since he's six months older. He didn't become a Geneva Redleg in Upstate New York until June 1960; I was already there. He outhit me by six points, but I outhomered him 18–1! The thing about Pete was that his memory was just unbelievable. He remembered the street where we lived, the name of the people whose house we lived in, and so much stuff about this small town in the now-defunct New York–Penn League. Running hard to first base on a walk was the only thing he could do well when he got to Geneva. He and Tony Perez spent another year in Class D. Two years in Class D baseball for Pete! He started to develop into the player he became. During the podcast, the only thing Pete and I talked about in regard to his issues with Major League Baseball was if he ever felt he was going to get into the Hall of Fame. He said, "I don't think about that much anymore." With his passing, who knows what will happen.

I interviewed actor Steve Schirripa (*Blue Bloods* and *The Sopranos*), *Everybody Loves Raymond* star Ray Romano, and producer Phil Rosenthal. I had an episode with dueling PR men from the Yankees and Mets: Marty Appel and Jay Horwitz (I usually interviewed one person at a time, but I thought it would be interesting to give the perspective of two teams in the same market). I talked to Mike Tannenbaum, the former Jets general manager who went on to ESPN. I spoke with Bobby Valentine while he was still the athletic director at Sacred Heart University. What I remember most about that interview is that he was standing up changing clothes (off-camera) because he had to go somewhere—and we talked about his managing career along with the story of his father-in-law, the late, great Ralph Branca. One of my favorite shows was with Branca's Brooklyn teammate Carl Erskine, who at 93 hadn't lost much off his mental fastball—he rattled off one-word descriptions of the whole Dodgers lineup. Oisk was from small-town Indiana, just like another old Dodger, Gil Hodges. Sadly, Carl passed at 97 in 2024.

I did more shows than I can recall, but I was glad Ron Swoboda and I spent time reminiscing about Tom Seaver after his death. Talking it out was good for both of us—and hopefully it helped some of the people out there listening too.

Former *New York Post* and *Newsday* writer Ken Davidoff and I did a couple of shows together. I had a few different editors help trim interviews down. It was a little bit of work and reminded me of my WFAN days. This time, though, I wasn't trying to serve lunch to a restaurant full of people while I was conducting interviews.

Cooperstown at Sea

The US Navy dedicated a freedom class combat ship named the USS *Cooperstown* on the West Side on the Hudson River in May 2023. I was there for the event, along with several other former teammates—including Ed Kranepool and Cleon Jones—plus the secretary of the navy, the governor of New York, several officials from MLB, and Johnny Bench, believe it or not. (I didn't remind him about banging up my car in Cincinnati 56 years earlier.)

It was the first naval ship named after Cooperstown, New York, which is, of course, home to the National Baseball Hall of Fame. The ship honors the 70 Hall of Famers who served the United States during wartime in conflicts spanning the Civil War, World War I, World War II, and the Korean War.

It was a pretty big thing and a beautiful ceremony. Naval brass, baseball brass, and government people were all there. Then on Sunday the Mets showed a video at Citi Field about the USS *Cooperstown* event. They had us come to the game and wave to the crowd for Gil, one of those 70 Hall of Fame veterans. It wasn't just for Gil; it was for all those who served. Whoever thought of the idea for the ship's naming should be congratulated. It was just a wonderful gesture.

Outfielder as the Relay Man

I love staying in touch with my friends, my teammates. I see myself as the person who lives in New York and is centrally located with everything going on. Everyone else pretty much lives outside the city. I like to check on people. I have an affinity for all my Mets teammates—especially the ones who were there in 1968, when Gil Hodges arrived and the attitude of the team changed. None of us saw what was coming.

Over the years I wanted to stay in touch with these people because they changed my life. I remember when Cal Koonce passed away in 1993; he'd been one of our veterans in the bullpen. He was the first one from the team who we lost. Of course, Gil had passed more than 20 years earlier. Danny Frisella, who pitched briefly for the '69 Mets and became an important member of the bullpen my last couple of years as a Met, died in an accident while still playing at age 30 in 1977.

Ed Charles was at Cal's funeral too, though I didn't know he'd be there until I got to the service. I was glad I went—I'm sure Ed felt the same way. And I remember meeting Cal's family in North Carolina. It was a beautiful family, and there was so much love for Cal, who was only 52—less than a year older than me at the time. Even though it was a sad day, I said to myself that I never want to lose touch with these guys because they've meant so much to me, my life, and my career. That's really my philosophy. I don't look at it as anything other than just staying on top of it and reaching out to my old friends.

I also touch base with many of their spouses. I recently checked in with Ron Taylor's wife. The good thing—as of the fall of 2024—is that he's still around, but the bad news is that he's in a home and doesn't recognize anybody. He's going through basically the same thing Buddy Harrelson went through until we lost him. Jim McAndrew's passing was a complete shock to me because of his health habits and how good he looked. And now, as this book is being written, the passings of Jerry Grote Bud Harrelson, and Ed Kranepool have really shaken all of us up.

There were guys who had already been with the Mets when I got there and had been through so much losing: Ed Kranepool, Tug McGraw, Ron Swoboda, and Al Jackson. Al and I weren't teammates long, and he was at the end of his career, but he really endured a lot in those early years: two 8–20 seasons for the fledgling Mets when he was pitching his heart out and getting no support—especially on defense.

In 1968 I was there when we finished ninth, a game ahead of Houston for last place. That gives you a little understanding of what's gone on with the club since 1962. There's a camaraderie you can't explain. So for me, my personal view is that I want to stay in touch with the guys. Always.

Miracle: Forever a Met

When I go out and talk in interviews and at events, the first thing that always comes up is the 1969 Mets. I am so proud to be associated with that team. There are really only two teams in the history of the game that people talk about years and years later. One of them is the 1927 Yankees, with Babe Ruth and Lou Gehrig, and the other is the 1969 Mets. People do talk about the 1919 Black Sox Scandal, when the Chicago White Sox were accused of throwing the World Series to the Cincinnati Reds. But the two teams people talk about *positively* are the '27 Yankees and the '69 Mets. It's been almost a century since Ruth hit 60 home runs in 1927 and the Yankees thoroughly dominated the field—they had been in the World Series the previous year and they'd be in the World Series again the next year, and many years to come. The 1969 Mets were a bolt of lightning, and that '69 team is the Miracle team that people talk about more than half a century later.

Miracle isn't a term of disrespect. Look where we came from the previous year: We finished ninth! And we barely finished ahead of Houston for last place. The Mets were considered the Lovable Losers for our first seven seasons of existence, losing 100 games almost every year, including 120 losses in 1962. It's hard to believe the White Sox lost 121 in 2024!

The 1977 movie *Oh, God!*, with George Burns in the title role, took Tom Seaver's 1969 quote about God being a Mets fan one step further. God (George Burns) comes to earth as an old man and befriends a grocery store manager, played by John Denver. God says, "The last miracle I did was the 1969 Mets. Before that, I think you have to go back to the Red Sea."

Fifty years from now, I don't think people will be talking about, say, teams from the 1980s or '90s. That's not to disparage those teams or anyone else, but you can't deny the fact that based on what was going on in the city, the country, and the world in 1969, and where our team had been in '68, the '69 Mets legacy resonates. More books have been written about that team than maybe any other sports team in history. I know! I've written two, and this is the third!

You could put together a lineup of all the players from that team who have written books focusing—for the most part—on 1969: Tom Seaver, Tug McGraw, Ed Kranepool, Donn Clendenon, Bud Harrelson, Cleon Jones, Ron Swoboda, Rod Gaspar, and me. Nolan Ryan and Tommie Agee also wrote books, though they did not focus on the 1969 team. Paul D. Zimmerman, best known for writing the Martin Scorsese film *The King of Comedy*, wrote the first book about the '69 Mets—*The Year the Mets Lost Last Place*—with writer and sports TV personality Dick Schaap; it was completed during the summer of 1969. That book came out two days after we won the World Series. Talk about good timing. I am writing this 100 years after the birth of our club's beloved manager, Gil Hodges, and it is a thrill to write that he is a Hall of Famer at last!

See? The '69 Mets are still breaking news. No other team has had that kind of publicity. Great underdog stories never get old—the kind of stories I only tell my friends.

Chapter 11

ADDITIONAL MIRACLES

'69 Mets Teammates

I have written about many of my Mets teammates throughout this book. I want to write something about everybody on the 25-man roster, whether I've already written about them or not. Everybody on that team played a role. If the 1969 team tells you anything, it's that it takes a team to shock the world and create something that still reverberates through the years. I'll remember it until my final day—Mets fans will never forget it, either.

Gil Hodges, Manager—Tough but fair. I always felt that if I got by his dressing room without him calling me in, then I was already ahead in the game!

Rube Walker, Pitching Coach—A true player's coach. Friendly with all the players. I always thought that if it were needed, Rube would have been the liaison between the players and Gil.

Yogi Berra, First Base Coach—Yogi and I had the St. Louis connection. I was told he was our hitting coach, but he *never* talked to me about hitting. I did say to him once, "Yogi, I'm struggling at the plate. What should I do?" He simply replied,

"See it and hit it." Nothing more had to be said. I never spoke to him about hitting again.

Ed Yost, Third Base Coach—The perfect coach. He was always willing to help make you better. The Walking Man—a nickname he picked up from his ability to draw a base on balls from his playing days. He knew how to get on base as a player and how to get a runner home as a coach. If you wanted to clone a third-base coach, it would be him.

Joe Pignatano, Bullpen Coach—Right out of Brooklyn. He loved and protected his bullpen guys. He was tough but someone you always wanted on your side.

Tom Seaver—A great pitcher but also a cutup on and off the field. A wonderful teammate. I called him the Vincent van Gogh of pitchers. Words can't describe how great a pitcher he was, but no doubt history will prove he was one of the best ever.

Jerry Koosman—If Seaver was Vincent van Gogh, then Koo was George Patton. Jerry was determined to defeat the enemy. If you needed a win, you could flip a coin, and whatever came up—Seaver or Koosman—you had a great chance of winning. On days he wasn't pitching, Koo was liable to be plotting a prank against a teammate or anyone else who came to his mind.

Gary Gentry—Great arm and good competitor. Overshadowed by Seaver and Koosman, he nevertheless pitched some great games in 1969. In retrospect I wish he would have taken better care of himself. Arm trouble and some personal demons took over, but he was fun to be around on and off the field.

Don Cardwell—Our number-four starter, Don was one of the few veterans on the 1969 team. He had been around for a while and could almost be considered an assistant coach to Rube Walker. Big Don was a great teammate on and off the field. I don't think any of us would ever want to physically mess with him even if he were fooling around. He pitched a no-hitter during his 14 seasons in the big leagues. He will always be remembered along with Jerry Koosman for the doubleheader in Pittsburgh in 1969 when both starters not only were the winning pitchers but each drove in the only runs in two 1–0 shutout victories.

Jim McAndrew—A quiet and unassuming but important pitcher for the Mets in 1969, Jim did a terrific job that year as a starter. Like some of us, the Iowa-born pitcher bore the brunt of Donn Clendenon's "critiques." He recently passed away, and I'll remember him as a great teammate.

Nolan Ryan—What can you say about Nolan? Like many on the '69 team, he was so young. He had a great arm but was saddled with military service that kept him away from the ballpark—and he was on a pitching staff that was one of the best in baseball. While he grew frustrated in New York, the trade to the Angels opened the door for him to have his Hall of Fame career. I have great memories of him throwing batting practice to us and pitching in late-afternoon games. You knew he was special—it was just a matter of time. Who can forget his terrific relief work in the playoffs vs. Atlanta and his great performance in Game 3 of the 1969 World Series? One of the greats I played with and against in my career.

Tug McGraw—Not sure words can describe the Tugger. I used to call him Frank. That was his real first name. He was a wonderful teammate. What a cutup! Separate from his pitching, he had the ability to keep everyone loose before, during, and after games. I have so many memories of his shenanigans on and off the field. Between him and Koosman, you had to be prepared for anything. He died way too young, but he's left an indelible mark with teammates and fans that has been passed on. "Ya Gotta Believe" in 1973 is one of his trademark sayings. He practically willed the Mets to that pennant that fall.

Ron Taylor—One of my favorite '69 Mets. I don't remember how he got his nickname, the Duke, as Boswell and I called him. He was not only a very good pitcher but one of the smartest people I knew. He was a working electrical engineer as a player, and after his baseball career, he went back to school in Canada and became a doctor. He ended up being the team physician for the Toronto Blue Jays for 36 years. I always told him I wouldn't ever let him check anything on me. Ron was the only Met in 1969 who had postseason experience, and it was vital in the playoffs and World Series. He never got the credit he deserved, but we all knew of his importance to the 1969 team.

Cal Koonce—Cal had a 6–3 record for the Mets in 1969, but he was also a veteran leader who was well-liked and very low-key. He died at an early age in 1993. I went to his funeral in North Carolina and was so impressed with his family; I realized all the good things about Cal were developed from his family roots.

Jack DiLauro—Pitched well for the 1969 Mets and—like another southpaw in the bullpen, Tug McGraw—started four games. I would call Jack the usual "crafty left-hander." He had a real sense of humor—and Jack did a great Ed Sullivan impersonation next to Ed the night we sang on the show.

Cleon Jones—One of my favorite teammates. Cleon was a terrific all-around player but truly one of the best hitters in baseball, particularly in 1969. His friendship with Tommie Agee going back to their youth in Mobile, Alabama, always made their conversations interesting. We were able not only to share great moments on the field but off the field, especially on the road.

Tommie Agee—Our center fielder was incredibly important to the 1969 Mets. His performance in Game 3 of the World Series was staggering: homering to lead off against future Hall of Famer Jim Palmer and not one but two Amazin' catches. I was in right field for the second catch, and all I remember is telling him he "had plenty of room." Tommie's death in 2001 at age 58 was a shock; he was way too young.

Ron Swoboda—Rocky was a great teammate and is still a close friend. Like Tug McGraw, he was liable to say anything to anyone at any time. I think he would admit it was to his detriment at times. We platooned in right field in 1969, and both of us always pulled for the other to succeed. His great catch in Game 4 of the '69 World Series is still talked about today and is one of the best ever.

Rod Gaspar—Rod readily admits he made the 1969 Opening Day roster because of my injured back. He never stopped thanking me for that. He has the nickname PP for reasons we don't ask about, yet I've been calling him that since I've known him. Rod, Wayne Garrett, and Ken Boswell were on *The Dating Game* right after we won the World Series. PP actually beat out Wayne and Kenny on the show; I tell him the girl wanted to walk off the stage when she saw it was him. I have never let Wayne and Kenny forget they lost to Rod on that show.

Ed Kranepool—Eddie was a really good player and had a long career in New York. He still holds some Mets records. He gave me the best advice when I first came over to the Mets. He told me, "When you go to all the breakfasts, lunches, dinners, and award events in NYC, always find a seat near an exit." Pretty sound advice from someone younger than me! I had lunch with him just days before he passed in 2024. Such a great friend.

Donn Clendenon—Donn was the guy who always was on somebody for something. He spared no one, but there were a few who felt his wrath more than others. I might have been one of them. A terrific addition to the '69 team in June, and no doubt we wouldn't have won without him. The MVP of the 1969 World Series hit crucial home runs in Games 2, 4, and 5. When he passed away in 2005, I said at a memorial for him, "The things I hated about him are the things I miss about him."

Ken Boswell—My roommate on the road. We were two people from different walks of life, but we became best of friends to this day. Kenny, like many others in 1969, was very young but was a key member of the '69 team. NYC wasn't too big for him, and he reaped the benefits of playing on that championship team and took it all in. I am thankful that we were put together as roommates—and platoon-mates, stationed on the same side of the diamond against right-handers—so we could share so many incredible moments on and off the field.

Al Weis—Mighty Mite was a great teammate and an essential member of the '69 team. His key hits in the World Series are still talked about today, and he will always be remembered as the ultimate team player.

Bud Harrelson—The glue of the Mets infield and a tremendous teammate.

Buddy was not a big man, but he was a big presence—both during his career and after he retired as a shortstop. He served as an announcer, coach, manager, and goodwill ambassador for the Mets and as co-owner and cofounder of the independent minor league Long Island Ducks. The world is not the same since we lost him.

Wayne Garrett—The youngest player on the 1969 team. Wayne was one of the lefty platoon players and even in his youth he was able to rise to the occasion in 1969. Whenever

I see him, he still looks like he is 21 years old to me. I'm sure why he wasn't the Mets third baseman for a long time.

Ed Charles—The Glider was the calming force in the clubhouse. His years of segregation and not being able to make it to the majors are a reflection of a horrible time in this country. Ed was able to calm us when things weren't going well and he also played an integral part as the oldest player on the team. He should have played another few years after 1969 but for some reason was phased out of the game. It was the Mets' and fans' loss!

Bobby Pfeil—He was an important utility player in 1969. With a number of players having military service during the year, Bobby was invaluable to the team. He had 211 at-bats during the season and was able to play second base, shortstop, and third base when needed. In Bobby's post-baseball life, he went into real estate development and became a huge success.

Jerry Grote—He was the best catcher I played with or against. Jerry could do it all—handle pitchers, throw out runners trying to steal, pop-ups, balls in the dirt, topped balls in front of the plate . . . all of it. He generally was pretty normal off the field, but once he saw the ballpark driving in or from the bus, his whole demeanor changed. He became very curt and at times difficult with the press. I believe his accomplishments were never written or talked about more because the press viewed him as a difficult person.

J. C. Martin—J. C. was one of a kind. He was a really good catcher and a great teammate. I never, ever heard him say a curse word, which is remarkable in a professional locker room. He was underrated defensively and a pretty good hitter. His bunt in Game 4 of the 1969 World Series, which led to Rod Gaspar scoring the game-winning run, is mentioned all the time when talking about that Series. That play proved how valuable everyone was and how everyone contributed on that team!

Duffy Dyer—One of the nicest players on the '69 Mets. The youngest of the three catchers Gil Hodges used, Duffy was a good defensive catcher and a good hitter. As a rookie, he only played in 29 games in 1969 but still contributed to the team's success—as did everyone on Gil's roster.

State of Mets

How many states did the Miracle Mets touch? Well, all 50, of course, plus anyplace where American military personnel were stationed (such as Vietnam), wherever expats were located, or anywhere people love New York or an underdog. But where did the Miracle Mets call home once they left Shea Stadium?

This list includes the birthplace of every Met who spent most of the year with the 1969 team. It includes the manager and coaches (*in italics*); Ron Taylor's native Canada is omitted, as it is obviously not a state. (Ron was the only '69 Met not born in the US.) Thanks to the addition of Gil Hodges and his coaches, 15 states are represented. Adding the Brooklyn-born coaching pair of Joe Pignatano and Eddie Yost helped New York match California as birthplace of the most 1969 Mets.

Some of the towns or states might not seem familiar because families move and hospitals are not always in the same place where a person grew up. The biggest surprise to me was Donn Clendenon's state of birth. I knew Donn came from Atlanta, but I had no idea he was actually born in my native Missouri. If I'd known that, I might have let him get on me even more than he already did.

Alabama: Tommie Agee (Magnolia), Cleon Jones (Plateau)
Arizona: Gary Gentry (Phoenix)

California: Rod Gaspar (Long Beach), Bud Harrelson (Niles), Tug McGraw (Martinez), Tom Seaver (Fresno)

Florida: Ed Charles (Daytona Beach), Wayne Garrett (Brooksville)

Indiana: *Gil Hodges (Princeton)*

Iowa: Jim McAndrew (Lost Nation)

Maryland: Ron Swoboda (Baltimore)

Minnesota: Jerry Koosman (Appleton)

Missouri: *Yogi Berra (St. Louis)*, Donn Clendenon (Neosho), Art Shamsky (St. Louis)

New Jersey: Bobby Pfeil (Passaic)

New York: Ed Kranepool (Bronx), *Joe Pignatano (Brooklyn)*, Al Weis (Franklin Square), *Eddie Yost (Brooklyn)*

North Carolina: Don Cardwell (Winston-Salem), Cal Koonce (Fayetteville), *Rube Walker (Lenoir)*

Ohio: Jack DiLauro (Akron), Duffy Dyer (Dayton)

Texas: Ken Boswell (Austin), Jerry Grote (San Antonio), Nolan Ryan (Refugio)

Virginia: J. C. Martin (Axton)

ACKNOWLEDGMENTS

Many people were helpful in completing this book, notably Marty Appel, Ken Boswell, Gil Hodges Jr., Jay Horwitz, Cleon Jones, Jerry Koosman, Ed Kranepool, Cabot J. Marks, Ken Samelson, Ed Schauder, James Snedeker, Ron Swoboda, Matt Winick, Toni McClelland, Terri Burkhart, Fred Cambria, and artist John Pennisi. We are grateful to literary agent Rob Wilson, Triumph Books acquisitions manager Josh Williams, Triumph editor Jeff Fedotin for putting this all together, project manager Katy Sprinkel Morreau, Laine Morreau, Bill Ames, director of author engagement, and everyone at Triumph who helped out but whose name might not appear in the boxscore. And Art's special thanks to Teresa Taylor for her love and belief in the project. Many thanks to the staff at Madman Espresso on 44th Street in Manhattan, where the authors frequently met and enjoyed good food, beverages, and banter during our many hours there in the writing process. Words can't adequately express our thanks to family and friends for their lasting support from the first at-bat to now.

While I think of all of the players I have played with over the years, I am particularly saddened by the deaths of my teammates of 1969. Over the years and recently I have lost so many of my close friends. What we accomplished as a team has become folklore. October 16, 1969 forever changed my life. What will never change are those relationships. and memories that will be with me forever.